Psychic Spellcraft

A WICCAPEDIA OF DIVINATION & INTUITION RITUALS

SHAWN
ROBBINS
&
LEANNA
GREENAWAY

STERLING ETHOS
New York

STERLING ETHOS
New York

Text © 2014, 2019, 2021 Shawn Robbins and Leanna Greenaway
Cover © 2021 Sterling Publishing Co., Inc.

Portions of this book were excerpted from *Wiccapedia* (2014), *The Crystal Witch* (2019),
and *The Witch's Way* (2019) by Shawn Robbins and Leanna Greenaway

This publication includes alternative therapies that have not been scientifically tested, is intended for informational
purposes only, and is not intended to provide or replace conventional medical advice, treatment or diagnosis or be a
substitute to consulting with licensed medical or health-care providers. The publisher does not claim or guarantee any
benefits, healing, cure or any results in any respect and shall not be liable or responsible for any use or application of any
content in this publication in any respect including without limitation any adverse effects, consequence, loss or damage
of any type resulting or arising from, directly or indirectly, any use or application of any content herein.

ISBN 978-1-4549-4388-4
ISBN 978-1-4549-4389-1 (e-book)

Distributed in Canada by Sterling Publishing Co., Inc.
c/o Canadian Manda Group, 664 Annette Street
Toronto, Ontario, Canada M6S 2C8
Distributed in the United Kingdom by GMC Distribution Services
Castle Place, 166 High Street, Lewes, East Sussex, England BN7 1XU
Distributed in Australia by NewSouth Books
University of New South Wales, Sydney, NSW 2052, Australia

For information about custom editions, special sales, and premium and corporate purchases,
please contact Sterling Special Sales at 800-805-5489 or specialsales@sterlingpublishing.com.

Manufactured in China

4 6 8 10 9 7 5

sterlingpublishing.com

Design by Sharon Jacobs and Shannon Nicole Plunkett
Cover design by Elizabeth Mihaltse Lindy
Picture credits—see page 295

To the seekers and believers, the explorers
of the universe, and beyond—you are the light
illuminating a world of mystery.
—*Shawn Robbins*

For Mamma Witch, who has shared so much
spiritual knowledge with me over the years, and
helped guide me through life's journey.
I owe everything to you.
—*Leanna Greenaway*

Contents

INTRODUCTION..................................... 1

PART ONE
Tapping into the Sixth Sense

1 Psychic Intuition and ESP........................ 6
2 Enhance Your Psychic Abilities................. 30

PART TWO
The Art of Divination

3 Scrying: Crystal Balls and Mirrors............. 60
4 Crystal Divination 82
5 Tarot Magick 106
6 Pendulum Divining 120
7 Palmistry....................................... 140
8 Botanomancy: Psychic Plant Power............ 158

9 From Aeromancy to Tea Leaf Reading:
  Other Forms of Divination 172

10 Numerology 198

PART THREE

Diving Deeper

11 Dreams and Astral Projection 236

12 Magickal Magnetism 254

13 The Spirit World 262

ACKNOWLEDGMENTS 294

PICTURE CREDITS 295

INDEX 297

Introduction

Believe it or not, everyone possesses psychic ability. Some might describe it as a good intuition, while others see it as a sixth sense. Whether you are a witchy-poo type or not, we are all born with an inner knowing. Have you ever had a bad feeling about something, but you ignore the warning signs and do the complete opposite? Often you will be proved right and end up saying to yourself, "I know I shouldn't have done that," or "I knew I shouldn't have trusted him."

Many witches believe these messages are given to us by our guides in the spirit world when it's necessary for them to intervene. We could be heading into a situation that isn't favorable or wander down the wrong path on our earthly journey. At times like these, our spirit helpers will speak directly to our subconscious, so in effect, we might get an odd feeling or have a compulsion to take a different route. It's like a little seed they plant in our mind or a gentle whisper in our ear.

When they want to steer us away from danger or direct us on the path that is chosen for us, they will communicate with us when we are sleeping so that we awake in a different frame of mind. They prefer to correspond with us when we are in a sleep state because when a human being sleeps, their subconscious is on an altered vibration. This makes it easier for them to connect with us. Clairvoyants and mediums can attain this altered state by achieving a positive meditation or relaxation.

We are all made up of energy, and most of the time, we can tap into and read another person's vibration. We might get a great feeling around certain people and a sinking or a sense of dread around others. Often in life, we are drawn to those folks who possess energy similar to our own, and this is why we choose to spend our lives surrounded by them. Just make sure that if those warning bells ever start to ring, you take notice!

Opening yourself up to your psychic abilities isn't easy. It can take many years to perfect, and even then, you will occasionally ignore the warning signs and end up in a situation that isn't pleasant. What many people don't realize is that spellcraft can really help in opening up any psychic blocks, leaving you free to receive information from the spiritual plane. If you are already psychic and perform types of divination regularly, you might be better at one practice than another. For example one of us (Leanna) is very adept at reading tarot cards and does well with psychometry, but struggles with the crystal ball, while the other (Shawn) is very adept at seeing into the future, but struggles with finding lost objects or pets. By working some witchcraft into your daily regime, you can strengthen certain abilities which enable you to tune into the task at hand. This book will hopefully give you lots of information to get you started on your journey. You can use so many tools as a crutch to harness your psychic energy, from pendulums to crystals and scrying mirrors to palmistry. Once you become skillful in one field, you can use try and practice with another. The more you work that psychic muscle, the better you will get at it, giving you the confidence to make your predictions with ease.

Part One

Tapping
into the
Sixth Sense

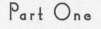

Chapter 1

Psychic Intuition and ESP

HAVE YOU EVER WISHED THAT YOU COULD SIT RIGHT where you are, in your comfy chair with a nice cup of tea, and know what's going on with your friends or family who are hundreds of miles away? Some Wiccans actually have the power to home in on the energy of distant places and events, and actually see them, through a skill known as *clairvoyance*. Others hear voices or impressions through *clairaudience* or feel energies through *clairsentience*. These kinds of ESP communications are far more interesting than telephoning your sister who lives down the street, and they're easy to achieve when you know how.

Even though we are talking about deliberately homing in on people or events that are close to your heart, many Wiccan seers can receive images, sounds, and feelings that they don't necessarily ask for, and often can't control, about people they don't know at all. For these Wiccans (Shawn included), this power can feel like a curse as well as a blessing. First, you can become very burdened with impressions you don't always understand; second, since most ordinary people tend to be skeptical, it is not always easy to get them to heed any warnings you might give them based on your insight.

This is not to say that we seers don't value and appreciate our gifts. We just have to learn to hone them, control them as best we can, and know when and how to put them to good use.

PSYCHICS AND SEERS THROUGH THE CENTURIES

Although their methods vary, those with fully developed clairvoyant abilities are able to open their minds and tap into psychic energies to see, hear, or know what others seemingly cannot. A psychic person often gets an overwhelming feeling that something is about to happen or they might receive these messages in a dream. A seer will physically see a vision either behind their closed eyes or in a divining object such as a crystal ball or a mirror.

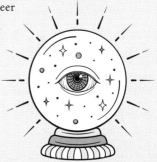

The term *psychic* comes from the Greek word *psychikos*, meaning "of the soul." In fact, somewhere in your schooling, you probably read or heard about the Delphic oracle, the famed priestess at the Temple of Apollo in Delphi, who would deliver predictions that purportedly came straight from Apollo. Was this telepathy? Clairaudience? We will never know . . . but we do know that the Greeks put a lot of trust in these revelations and looked to such oracles to deliver news from the future on a regular basis.

However, historical ESP isn't limited to the ancient Greeks. The Bible is filled with prophets warning the masses of things to come. Some people listened, some ignored them, and some became true believers when these visions came to fruition. Some believe that religious prophets

throughout history received messages from a divine source; others believe that such people were actually receiving messages from the other side. It is possible that these gifted people were receiving some kind of spiritual message that was invisible and inaudible to others. Therefore, it is quite conceivable they possessed some kind of intuitive skill that enabled them to see and hear what wasn't apparent on the physical plane. Joan of Arc can be seen as an example: although Christians view her visions as divine prophecies, she wouldn't have been seeing anything without a heightened state of awareness, which can certainly be categorized as ESP.

Nostradamus (1503–66), perhaps the most famous seer in history, began his professional life as a physician in France. After his wife and child died of the plague, he fell apart, to be reborn as a teller of the future. He is, of course, the author of the famed book *The Prophecies*, which his followers believe has predicted everything from the assassination of Lincoln to the rise of Hitler to 9/11. Some people question whether Nostradamus was clairvoyant or a prophet. There's no real scholarly answer to this. As far as I'm concerned, prophets *are* seers, so I would say that he was both.

One famous modern-day American seer was Edgar Cayce (1877–1945), also known as "the sleeping prophet," since many of his visions came to him while he was resting quietly in a trance-like state. When someone with a problem asked Cayce for guidance, the seer would lie down and put himself into a trance and then report his findings to an assistant who was taking notes at his side. Cayce, who believed firmly that the subconscious mind held information not available to the conscious mind, claimed not to remember his visions or what he had told his assistant, but the accuracy of some of his predictions gained him a large following of supporters.

In 1972, researchers Harold Puthoff and Russell Targ conducted a series of studies on remote viewing at the Stanford Research Institute designed to determine whether seers could give precise information about distant locations or persons. Puthoff and Targ chose random locations and then asked the seers to tune in to those spots and either verbally describe or sketch what they were seeing. Three men (including the famed psychic Uri Geller) were determined to have clairvoyant skills. Of course, some skeptics grumbled and called the experiment a farce, but that is nothing new.

EXTRASENSORY EXPERIENCES

Within each and every one of us is a power far greater than anyone can imagine. This is called a sixth sense, and although everybody has it, not everyone knows how to access it. Think about a time when you just knew what the outcome of an event would be, without a question in your mind. Whether you acknowledge it or not, you were leaning on your intuition. Most of us have natural skills of premonition, but many ignore these visceral feelings, opting to rely on logic and reasoning instead. Those people who have mastered the art of tapping into the sixth sense have a natural ability to recognize otherworldly energies around them.

Just like animals, we are all born with a natural ability to detect when a situation feels "off." For example, we rarely see wild animals in the path of a tsunami; they usually sense something is amiss and make for higher ground.

This sense of premonition tends to be socialized out of humans, starting from an early age. Little children can innately identify spirits,

primarily because they are not long from the spirit realm and often have a guide close by. For kids, it is natural to state, "I see Grandma on the couch," when Grandma died more than a year ago, but most ordinary families discourage this kind of behavior and put it down to the child being eccentric. Children learn very quickly to suppress these abilities, and over time, because they don't use it, they lose it.

ESP, or extrasensory perception, is a wide-ranging term often used when talking about a sixth sense. Many other phenomena comprise the sixth sense, too, such as any heightened feelings relating to our other five senses. Here are some of the different kinds of gifts that are involved, and the various energies that people (including you) may be sensitive to:

Clairvoyance

This is the ability to see energies, events, or entities that aren't visible to most people. Mediums often experience clairvoyance when the spirits of those who have passed on appear during a divination, or when they can envision something that happened to you in the past—or something that is going to happen in the future. Clairvoyants receive visions either while in a state of meditation, while asleep, or while they're going about their daily business.

Clairalience

Psychic information relayed by scent is clairalience. This is different than a memory being sparked by a smell—we all have a strong connection to

certain scents from childhood or strong emotional experiences. Clairalience involves more of a "phantom" scent—something that only the intended recipient can detect. For example, some people experiencing hauntings will say they smell something putrid or, conversely, that they smell perfume or something similarly singular to a nearby spirit. A psychic who helps with police investigations may smell orange blossoms, indicating that the subjects of a manhunt are hiding out in an orange grove. Or, more commonly, you may catch a whiff of your long-dead grandfather's cologne or cigar smoke, indicating that his spirit is nearby.

Clairaudience

Clairaudience is the ability to hear psychic communications, though it's not like hearing a low vibration or a high-pitched dog whistle. These may be the voices of spirit guides or messages from spirits who have passed. Some of the voices may not make sense without more information. Why are you hearing an old woman's voice whenever your friend Mary is visiting? It could be her grandmother who recently passed away.

Claircognizance

Claircognizants don't hear or see images, and yet they know things that they couldn't possibly have learned through everyday means. For example, a claircognizant may be able to tell you who your great-great-great-grandfather was, even though he's never heard the man's name before and has no background on your family history. The claircognizant himself doesn't know how this information found its way into his consciousness; it just pops out of his mouth.

Clairsentience or Clairempathy

Clairsentients can assess and feel the energetic fields around people and other beings—animals, plants, or anything with a life force—and shift those energies if need be. People who have this ability very intensely are known as empaths, and they must learn to protect their spiritual space, as it is very easy to become inundated by pain, fear, anxiety, or other negative emotions. Most of us can easily sympathize with other people, but empaths feel the *exact* same happiness or pain as another person, or even an animal. People with empathetic powers must be careful not to absorb the energies of everyone around them, as this can be overwhelming and, at times, depressing. Psychics with these abilities must sometimes take time away from other people in order to protect and restore their own energy.

Mediumship

There is a difference between ESP and mediumship. All mediums have ESP, but not all people with ESP can communicate with the deceased and so are not mediums. Some mediums' ability to talk with spirits occurs from childhood; others say they became aware of their skill later in life.

Mediums can often see, smell, hear, and feel deceased people and spirits of all forms. People who have true mediumistic gifts are rare. Some profess to have the ability when in fact they might just have a conglomeration of the capabilities listed here. See Chapter 13 for more helpful information.

Precognition

This involves having knowledge of an incident before it happens, whether through a vision or a dream. This is a little different from a premonition, which is the feeling that something good or bad is about to happen. A precognitive soul is someone who says, "Don't get on that train—it's going to derail!" Premonition is more like "I have an uneasy feeling about your upcoming trip." People with precognition have predicted global disasters, plane crashes, and even future presidents.

Telepathy

Telepathy is communicating or sharing visions or feelings with someone without speaking. This is not the same as catching your best friend's eye in a crowded setting and knowing that you're both amused by the same thing. Telepathy is *knowing* that your brother is distressed, even though you live across the country and haven't spoken to him in a while. See pages 26–29.

THE GIFT OF CLAIRVOYANCE: SHAWN'S STORY

Since I was a child, I have the gift of clairvoyance—a skill that has not always been welcome in my life. Let me tell you my story.

My grandmother, an unusual and lovely woman, sat me down one day when I was very young and said, "Shawn, you know you're different, don't you?" I knew that I was, even at that age, but still, because I had no words to describe how I felt or how exactly I was different from other kids, I asked what she meant. She told me I was clairvoyant, explaining, "You know things others don't. You can see things before they happen. You can read what other people are thinking, can't you?"

She was right. I could do all of those things, at least sometimes, but being so young, I thought that everybody could! This was the first time my gifts were laid out on the table before me, so to speak, and I had to acknowledge and accept them as something that set me apart from my friends, something that I had and they didn't.

Just a couple of weeks after this conversation with my grandma, I was playing with my friends when I heard her voice saying good-bye to me, telling me that she'd be seeing me in heaven. You can imagine how upsetting this would be for anyone, let alone a little girl! I ran to my mother and asked what had happened to my grandmother, and I learned that she had been admitted to the hospital. By the end of the day, we got the call that Grandma had passed away.

This is just one of hundreds of messages I've received since my childhood, and that time it was very precise. Other times, though, I've gotten false alarms. I once believed that someone I knew was going to die in a horrible car accident, and I cried and cried and cried all through the day. I found out later that night that she had arrived home safe and sound, and then I had to face the fact that my premonitions weren't always correct. I wasn't sure how I felt about this; I didn't know if I had been flat-out wrong or if I had misinterpreted what I saw, but I was, of course, relieved that she was unharmed.

This kind of misguided intuition can often happen with psychics. Most people have deep-seated fears for their loved ones at one time or another, but when you have the "gift" it is hard to differentiate between your fear and a real message. The psychic wires can get crossed, and then it's easy to lose faith in your ability.

How to Relay Difficult Messages

If you have psychic abilities, what should you do when you see something scary or negative in a person's future? Is it helpful to tell the person, or is that something you should keep to yourself? On the one hand, if you can tell the person about something they can prevent—like getting hit by a bus—it may be wise to give a warning. On the other hand, if you see long-term illness or extreme sadness, it becomes a little more complicated. Should you tell, or should you sit there smiling, as if everything were hunky-dory?

We are believers in telling the truth, no matter what, but you also have to remember that you are not God and you won't wake up psychic every morning. You have to be tactful and choose your wording very carefully. Also, sometimes the messages we get can be vague or jumbled up, so it's not always the case that you can clearly see your friend or loved one becoming seriously ill or being hit by a bus. Often, you'll just get a message that your friend may need to see a doctor for some reason or that they may experience back pain—nothing too scary to foretell—but later you'll discover how accurate you were when you hear that your friend slipped on ice, hurt their back, and had to see the doctor.

So in the event that you have negative news to report, always be sensitive, and think before you speak. Give a warning without terrifying the life out of your friend, and remember these truths:

- **We all have free will.** Just because you are seeing something in the future that *could* happen, it doesn't mean that it *will* happen. The future is changing all the time, based on our actions and the actions of other people. It's like the Butterfly Effect—one small incident can set off a chain reaction of other incidents, so nothing is ever really set in stone.

- **The trials in our lives lead us to acquire greater strength and open new doors.** Although it does not seem like a good thing at the time, something that seems like a huge tragedy right now—the end of a marriage, the loss of a job—might just be the beginning of a new future. Always give hope and tell people they are learning valuable lessons and being guided by their angels.

- **When someone comes to you with a big problem** and they have nowhere else to turn, help keep their feet on the ground by telling them that the Divine Creator never gives people anything they can't cope with. Instill your strength into them and encourage them with new ideas.

When you're working with your own skills, it's important to remember that your feelings, and the visions and sound impressions you receive, don't *make* things happen. Nothing you see, hear, or sense will be your fault. People with powers of ESP sometimes feel very guilty when their negative premonitions come to pass. Sometimes you can warn people, sometimes you can't, and often they won't listen. So take things as they come, use your best judgment as to sharing the information, and then learn to let it go.

Telling What You See

Through years of practice and repetition, I've learned how to "call up" visions for other people. If someone comes to me for advice on a particular issue, I can focus enough to "see" what's going to happen.

For example, if a woman came to me asking whether she should keep seeing a certain man, I would close my eyes and enter into a deep meditative or trance-like state while focusing on the question. A date might pop into my mind, in which case I would tell her to mark her calendar and look for something significant to happen; or it might be a location such as a restaurant, in which case I would probably advise her that it could be the site of a significant night on the town with her gentleman friend; or I might actually see a proposal or a breakup.

Like Edgar Cayce, I tend not to remember the trances or what happened during them. A clairvoyant's subconscious mind tends to block out our encounters and leave us with a sense of amnesia. This may be a defense mechanism to keep us from getting overly spooked by things that are unexplained. But I'm always happy to assist whenever and wherever I can, and once you come to develop your ability, I know you will be too!

Clairvoyance and Crime Solving

For all the skepticism surrounding ESP, every now and then you'll hear that a police agency has turned to a clairvoyant for help in cracking a case. Often this is in connection with a missing person, but sometimes a seer will come into a violent crime scene as well.

Seers, whether they consider themselves clairsentient or not, can use, and actually depend on, the energy from the target (in this case, the missing person or the perpetrator) or the crime scene itself to glean valuable information. When I've helped the police solve crimes, I have gone directly into the crime scene. It gives off vibrations that help me to envision what went on there and who might be responsible.

When someone commits an act of violence, they leave behind a heap of negative energy. This is kind of like leaving DNA behind, but the authorities can't dust for energy and bag it up like other evidence. If I can connect with that energy, I can get a read on who this person might be, what their current energetic state might be (are they scared? still angry? dead?), and even where they might be. (Do I see or feel a cold, wet, dark place? Might they be in a boathouse or a shipyard?) This is really a form of clairsentience leading me into clairvoyance.

Likewise, when a person has gone missing, it is helpful for the seer to either go to the scene of the abduction (if it's known) or turn to psychometry and to physically hold something that belongs to the person. The item, whatever it is, will help the seer connect to the missing person's current state of energy and perhaps receive a vision of where the person is now.

It is frustrating when skeptics say, "Oh, anyone could give such a vague description of a place!" First, it's better information than any non-seer could provide; second, a vague description is still better than nothing at all, and it does provide some direction for the authorities.

Most seers genuinely want to share their ability to help; most are not out to get famous or to score their own reality shows. They've been born with a skill that can feel like a blessing and a curse, and they want the blessings to far outweigh any negativity they've had to deal with.

A number of years ago I worked in the government-funded CIA Stargate Project during the Cold War. I trained psychics who, like me, had extraordinary extrasensory perception (ESP). I felt my call to duty had changed from being a prophet of doom to saving the world from harm. We were schooled in the art of remote viewing, receiving training in how to enter the alpha state.

The alpha state is a higher, trancelike state of being achieved through the power of the mind, where the sixth sense is enhanced and psychic abilities reach higher awareness. Entering the alpha state was a skill held by many of the mystics of yesteryear. We hope to enable you to trust and believe in yourself, open your heart and soul, and use your newfound psychic gifts for the betterment of humankind.

Developing Clairvoyance with Your Third Eye

Let's say that you suspect you have clairvoyant abilities. How can you develop them? Is there a school for seers? There actually are seminars for sharpening this skill, but you can also try to do it in the privacy of your own home.

Experts in the field will tell you that clairvoyance is the result of having a clear, open "third eye." A little background may be needed if you aren't familiar with the term: the third eye is part of the body's chakra system. The sixth chakra, the location of the third eye, is in the middle of the forehead (though it might be higher or lower on some people); it is related to intuition and a higher understanding of the world.

The first thing you can do to improve your clairvoyance is to make sure that your third eye chakra is clear. This can be done through a special meditation for which you'll need a blue crystal or a gemstone.

MATERIALS

A blue crystal or a gemstone such as azurite, lapis lazuli, or kyanite

1 or more tealight candles

Soothing music

RITUAL

Dim the lights, light the candles, and start playing the music. Now lie down and place the blue crystal or stone on your forehead. Breathe deeply—inhale through the nose as deeply as you can, then blow out through the mouth. Breathe in and out this way for 30 to 60 seconds. Start to focus on the area where the crystal is. Imagine the crystal opening up that space. Maybe you'll feel a warming or tingling sensation.

When you're feeling like the space is wide open, make sure you are still breathing deeply. Unfocus your mind and see whatever comes to you. You don't have to know what the vision is about; you can interpret that part later. For the time being, just be with the vision for the moment.

Here's where you can also try to develop clairaudient capabilities. While you're in your deep meditative state, take some time to focus on your ears as well. See if you can hear anything coming to you from the other side.

Blue Mood

To enhance your powers of clairvoyance when you practice, always wear a piece of the royal blue stone lapis lazuli (for example, as part of a necklace or a ring) next to your skin. It can also be worn outside of practice to attract visionary vibrations. Once you get into the swing of tapping into your own clairvoyance, visions of forthcoming events will pop into your mind sporadically. Although at first these visions will just seem like your imagination running away with you, you'll gain more confidence in your capabilities once they start coming true.

PSYCHOMETRY:
TOUCH ME, FEEL ME, READ ME

Psychometry is one form of ESP that some Wiccans use, and one that many people find especially intriguing. It's the ability to hold an object that belongs to someone else and get a "read" on that person. On pages 20–21, we discussed psychics helping to solve crimes. In such cases, we'll often be asked to hold something that belongs to a missing person or a suspect in the hope that we'll pick up a sensation or emotion that will be helpful in the investigation.

It's quite possible that you've experienced psychometry yourself without realizing it.

Have you ever worn a piece of vintage clothing or jewelry and felt anxious or just "off" somehow? It wasn't because the crinoline was scratching you or the diamond was blinding you; it was probably because the person who wore it before you had the same sense of nervousness. Cloth and metal are "absorbent" elements; clothes and jewelry act like psychic sponges and can soak up vibrations from their wearers. These vibrations—happy or unhappy energies, depending on the owner—often hang around for centuries, so antique objects especially are pervaded with them.

Now, this might send you heading for the hills, but the vibrations can be especially strong if the clothing or jewelry was worn by someone who was dying (or who actually died) while wearing it. This is true only if the person was not at peace about passing to the next plane, though. Clothing and accessories that come from people who are ready to move on are usually cloaked in a sense of serenity and peace.

You should *never* pass down engagement or wedding rings or wedding gowns to your children or grandchildren if you got divorced or were unhappy in your marriage. It's asking for trouble!

You can also use psychometry to get a good first impression of a person. Have you ever read the Stephen King book *The Dead Zone*, which was also made into a film and later a television show? The main character, Johnny Smith, has the ability to touch people and see their future. For him, this usually involves a vision of a fiery death, a nuclear war, or involvement in a heinous crime—but don't let that turn you off. It's far more common to use psychometry to get a general feel for someone or for your surroundings than to visualize a dramatic disaster.

So how do you put this psychic sense to work?

1. **Practice with a friend.** When you meet up for lunch or a shopping date, ask her not to tell you anything about how her day has gone so far, then take her hand as though you're going to shake it. Close your eyes and focus on the energy you're picking up.

2. **Let your senses really speak to you.** Are you picking up a chill? Does your head suddenly ache? Are you feeling warm suddenly?

3. **Interpret these feelings.** For example, is it possible your friend just got over the flu? Remember that feelings don't have to be literal, although you certainly could receive something pretty straightforward. You might also receive a sense of general discomfort, which is harder to interpret but definitely gives you an idea of what's going on with your friend.

As you hone this skill, you can use it to help you gain insight during business dealings and personal interactions. Simply shaking hands with a colleague or associate can give you a heads-up as to what the other person is all about! Find out if your neighbor is on the up-and-up. Know with one (innocent) touch if your blind date is worth your trouble. You can do all this with one hand tied behind your back—you just need the other hand free to do some investigating.

BRAIN TELEGRAMS
AND TELEPATHIC MESSAGES

Fans of the *Star Wars* movies know that the Jedi had some serious mind skills going on, namely, in the form of telepathy—sending and receiving thought waves. Some people call this reading minds, others call it communicating without speaking. Whatever you call it, telepathy is awfully convenient, especially if you're in a crowded room and you don't feel like shouting.

We've all had our telepathic moments. Maybe you've been talking with a friend and known exactly what she was going to say before she opened her mouth, or maybe you've both said the same thing at the same time. This is the result of being on the same thought wavelength. As you already know, this is easily achieved with some people (your best friends or loved ones, for example), but not so easily with others (your standoffish boss).

Since you can use telepathy to your advantage, especially in the case of a boss or coworker you just can't relate to, it is an important skill to have in your psychic toolbox. To learn to send and receive telepathic messages,

you're going to need a willing and open-minded friend, preferably one you've shared mind waves with in the past. Once you get the hang of using brainwaves, you'll be able to work on your own. For now, get together with that friend and follow these steps:

1. **Relax.** Regular meditation and visualization (discussed later in this chapter and in other chapters) are essential to warming up your telepathic tendencies. There are parts of your brain that need to be open to the possibilities that surround you; if they're closed, you can forget about picking up or sending messages through the ether. So before you begin, allow time for you and your lovely assistant to sit back and chill your minds for ten or fifteen minutes.

2. **Decide which of you will be the sender** and which will be the receiver. For the sake of this discussion, you're going to be the sender.

3. **When you're both relaxed, visualize an image that you want to send.** Let's say you're transmitting the thought of a basketball. Really make it real in your mind: the perfect roundness, the knobby, rubbery material, even the smell. It's best to start with an image instead of a thought, because an image is one compact package that isn't subject to getting lost in translation, the way a phrase might be. When you perfect your skill, you'll be able to send and receive thoughts as well.

4. **Picture a tube running between your brain and your friend's.** Now, send that basketball down the tube. Hold the picture clearly and steadily in your mind as your friend retrieves the image.

This technique takes practice to perfect. Even though you and your pal might be similarly minded, you haven't been purposely accessing these parts of your minds up to this point. So be patient, pour one glass of wine if you like, and have fun with it! (Drinking more than one glass can dull your senses.)

Once you really get the hang of telegraphing with the mind, put it to use when you need it most: in your yearly review at work (send the message "I'm a great worker, and you need to pay me more!"); on a hot date (try "Notice how beautiful and smart I am!"); or even when you take your car in for service (something along the lines of "You are going to be honest and not overcharge me for this work!"). Try to put it to use in as many everyday situations as you can and just wait for the benefits to come back to you. Keep in mind, though, that negative or dishonest thoughts should never be telegraphed—this can invite negative energy and create bad karma.

Chapter 2

Enhance Your Psychic Abilities

WHEN WE TALK ABOUT PSYCHIC SKILLS, WE ARE TALKING about the ability to process input and information that is all around us all the time. Some of this information is visible and obvious, while other signs are subtle and easily missed. We are all born with a sensitive intelligence and enough spirituality to process intangible universal cues, but as we age, most of us become focused on other things happening in our daily lives and lose our belief in the energies that we can't see. Intuition is strongly linked to our psychic ability, and both are useful in divination.

We are all born with an inner voice that tells us when a situation or person is good, bad, or dangerous, but with time, many of us tune out that voice and try to reason our way through life. While reason certainly has its place, it does fall short sometimes. Think about a time when you just knew someone was lying to you but you couldn't prove it, or when you met a person for the first time and took an immediate dislike to them. In the absence of actual evidence to validate your feelings, you reasoned, *This person must be telling the truth* or *Everyone else thinks this person is fabulous, so it must be me.* And then, of course, the truth was eventually exposed, and you learned that your intuition was right! Never ignore your feelings. If a thought pops into your head, it must be for a reason.

Fortunately, intuition is never really lost. In fact, it's rather easily recovered with a little effort. Once your intuition is up and running, we can dig into some psychic tricks!

LIGHT UP YOUR INTUITION

Here's a simple visualization exercise to get your intuition moving. First, clear your mind of the distractions you've been dealing with all day long. Take the phone off the hook and give the dog a bone to keep him occupied for the next fifteen minutes.

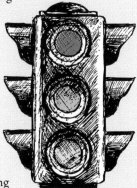

Next, make a list of questions you need answers to—anything from "Is this stock a sound investment?" to "Is my health going to improve soon?" Tailor your questions to your concerns. You'll use this list a bit later in the exercise.

Now close your eyes. Breathe deeply but keep your mind clear—you're not focusing on or analyzing anything, just clearing out the psychic clutter. Imagine a traffic light just as it would appear in real life—red at the top, yellow in the middle, green at the bottom. Start warming up your instincts by asking practice questions. For example, ask, "Is my hair blond?" and see what color lights up in your mind. You should use the three traffic light colors that you envision as your answers: Red is no. Green is yes. Yellow indicates maybe or uncertainty. Ask some other questions you know the answers to, such as:

"Am I a woman?"

"Is it Saturday?"

"Is it the year 2045?"

These kinds of questions will give you a base reading to go on. Ask a question that will give you a "maybe" response, too, since that's always a possible answer.

At this point you're ready to get down to your main concerns. Don't think—just ask. What color appears? That's your answer, and that's all there is to it!

Body Language

Your body's reaction is an integral part of your intuition, so start listening to what it's telling you. Sometimes we want something so much that we avoid obvious signals. If you've recently made a decision and you feel anxious and jittery, don't write that off as nervous excitement. It could be that your body is reacting to what it knows is a bad choice, desperately trying to warn you. On the other hand, a feeling of peace or a surge in positive energy could indicate that you *are* following your intuition and your physical systems are feeling serene as a result. If anxiety is driving you mad over a decision you've made, try clearing your mind and using the traffic-light method on pages 31–32 to see if you're really on the right track or if you're headed for an unfortunate detour.

Dreaming of Better Intuition?

Your dreams are one of the best indicators of your intuition. This is because when you dream, you are using your subconscious mind instead of your conscious mind, which is often cluttered with alternative plans, fears about the future, and that pesky thing called logic.

It's easy to be confused by dreams, though, since a lot of intuitive information comes through in the form of symbols that can seem bizarre to the untrained interpreter. Chapter 11, on dreams, will give you an overview of how to decode your overnight happenings, and you can always go online for help interpreting any symbols not listed there.

Start keeping a dream journal to help you follow what your mind is telling you, especially if you're going through an especially troubling or difficult time. Your mind *wants* to give you the advice you need! Take it, follow it, and rest easy.

Stop Analyzing!

The most important thing about trusting your instinct is to just go with it. This can be an incredibly difficult task for people who need to analyze every thought they have and every move they make. While there's something to be said for planning and organizing the long-term aspects of your life, there are many things that are out of your control. Life is going to do what it's going to do, and you just have to roll with it sometimes.

For instance, if you're using your intuition to figure out whether or not you should buy a specific house, and it's a house that you really, really want—and your intuition is saying, "This is not the place for you!"—then you have to be willing to accept that. Don't try to figure out why your mind is working against your wants, just trust that there's a reason. When you rely on your intuition, you'll never be sorry. Your inner compass is not making up new directions for you to follow, it is just steering you down the path you already know you should be on.

TRUST YOUR INTUITION

Once you start tuning in to your senses on a regular basis, you'll be able to rely on your intuition to guide you through any situation. There are some people who tell me, "My intuition is always wrong! I should just do the opposite of my gut feeling!" These people aren't lacking in intuition; they simply need more practice in sensory training. I suspect they made a poor decision once or twice (probably by going against their gut feeling) and now they're just flummoxed whenever they have an important choice to make. Their senses are in confusion, and their decision-making process is the psychic equivalent of throwing a dart at a board while blindfolded. What do I say to these people? "Take off the blindfold already!" Yes, it really *is that simple.*

So let's say you are one of these people whose intuition is all twisted up in reason and logic and "what-ifs." How can you clear out the cobwebs and get back to acknowledging and trusting your instincts?

1. **Start with a simple decision,** something like "Should I drive down Main Street or South Street on my way to work today?"

2. **One answer will pop into your mind.** Make a note of it. That's your gut feeling. Don't think about it, don't look for logical reasons, don't argue with yourself.

3. **Breathe in and out, deeply and quietly,** and just let that answer sit. Be confident in your decision to trust your intuition. Push all waffling feelings aside.

4. **Now do it.** Take the street your intuition chose. Don't be disappointed if your drive goes less than smoothly. If you encounter problems on your way to work (traffic, construction, whatever), that doesn't necessarily mean your intuition was wrong; it could mean that you avoided an accident on the other route—one that didn't happen since you weren't there. So don't throw

your hands up and say, "I chose wrong *again*! My intuition is good for nothing!" It's nice when we have a solid positive outcome to hang the intuitive hat on, but we can't always see or know what *didn't* happen because of the choice we made.

Then again, sometimes it's obvious that we've made the wrong decision, like trusting the wrong person, buying the wrong house, or taking the wrong job. If you took the time to check in with your intuition and you think it steered you wrong, let's take a look at your process. Did you ask:

> **"Should I date this person?"**
>
> **"Should I buy this house?"**
>
> **"Should I take this job?"**

If so, you may need to get more specific the next time around. There are always lessons—good or bad—to be learned in any life situation, so when you ask if you "should" do something, the answer could easily be, "Hey, why not?" But to learn whether something will bring you more happiness than sorrow, you could ask:

> **"Is this person honest and loyal?"**
>
> **"Will I be happy living here?"**
>
> **"Will I grow and prosper in this job?"**

Try this rephrasing process and go with the first answer that pops into your mind. And trust yourself. You know more than you think you do!

Listening to Intuition

To reacquaint yourself with your inner voice, you need to give yourself the time and space to actually hear it. A few crystals, such as benitoite, euclase, kyanite, moonstone, or hollandite, can really help unlock your hidden intuition.

Find a quiet spot where you can sit or lie comfortably for ten to fifteen minutes, and cup your chosen crystal in your hands. Think about an issue in your life that is causing some confusion (like the previous example of someone lying to you but insisting they are telling the truth). Allow yourself to feel the emotions that come to you when thinking about this issue. You might feel tense, angry, sad, etc. Don't fight these feelings or even try to understand them, as this is getting into the realm of using reason. Just let them wash over you.

Now listen to that voice telling you what the truth is—not what you wish it to be and not what someone else has told you about it. Trust that your intuition is on the right track.

This is a skill that needs to be practiced and honed, especially if you've ignored your perceptions for some time. Some people have trouble

determining what they feel about a situation when they start this process, but keep at it—intuition is like riding a bike. It will come back to you if you let it!

OPENING THE PSYCHIC DOOR

Many people assume that Wiccans are "seers"—that we have the ability to see and sense what others simply cannot, because of our connection to nature, or the devil, or the cosmos, or what have you. (The devil definitely has nothing to do with it as Wiccans do not believe that the devil exists!) The truth of the matter is that we are better able to tune in to what may happen, or what may already be happening where we can't see it, but the reason is simply that we have a deep connection to our intuition. We listen to it, we follow it, we rely on it.

Our prehistoric ancestors depended heavily on their instincts and intuition, which they used to respond to everything from changes in climate to the presence of predators or prey. Over time, many of us in the Western world have lost touch with this ability and come to disregard that part of our internal makeup. But everyone is born with ESP, or extrasensory perception. We all experience gut feelings and hunches; if we only listened to these feelings a little more, we could avoid many of the problems we find ourselves facing on a day-to-day basis. Have you ever met someone for the first time and felt the hair on the back of your neck stand on end? I know I have. Although the person may seem charming enough, your first impression, as incongruous as it may be, can often be right. This is your sixth sense kicking in, and it should never be ignored. Whether you believe it or not, you *are* psychic. Each and every person residing on this planet has some level of psychic ability, whether their psychic "door" is wide open, tightly closed, or left ajar.

If you were raised in a culture where intuitive abilities were encouraged and honed, you'd be in touch with them all of the time, but unfortunately, we Westerners are told from an early age that if you can't see it, it doesn't exist. Any child who claims to see spirits, or who just *knows* things (like a little girl who always says, "Grandma's about to call" just before the phone rings), is dismissed as having an overactive imagination and told to stop exaggerating and "tell the truth!"

The situation is not helped by the hundreds of so-called psychics out there who are quick to con the general public out of a few bucks in order to line their own pockets. Leanna and I are both natural clairvoyants and travel in many different psychic circles, and we have both come up against these professional charlatans who, sadly, give the rest of us a bad name. A genuine mystic can spot a bogus psychic a mile away, but some susceptible folk may not realize they are being conned until it's too late.

Psychic abilities take many forms. The term *ESP* is often used as a catchall phrase to cover everything from heightened intuition to clairvoyance, clairaudience, psychometry, telepathy, dowsing, precognition, scrying, and mediumship. After you have read this chapter, you'll be more aware of your particular psychic abilities. We all have our own strengths and weaknesses, so don't be surprised to learn that some of your abilities are better developed than others.

By now, you're probably thinking, "Hey, I want to start using my ESP! How do I find these gifts?" First, relax. It's going to take a little work to uncover them and get them revved up again!

Prime Your Psychic Pump

No one—not even a Wiccan—can just jump into psychic living after years of being shut down. You have to ease into it gently by reminding the right side of your brain of its limitless capabilities. So the first step in finding your ESP is to acknowledge that you have the power to access information that was previously hidden from you. To do this, I suggest you start every day by reminding yourself of this fact. A simple affirmation or mantra will do, something like "My brain is wide open and ready to receive information."

The next thing you should do is to begin researching. Start with metaphysical bookstores, where you'll most likely find not only a wealth of materials, but staff who are eager to share their knowledge and experience with you. This is a good place to ask about nearby Wiccan or psychic groups. The Internet, of course, is another excellent research tool. Google "improve your psychic skills" or "Wicca psychic abilities" and see what pops up.

Learning as much as you can about a given psychic ability, especially one you feel you have an affinity for, will help you understand what you're dealing with and how to get the most out of it. In fact, narrowing down the field of psychic possibilities is a good starting point. Learn your strengths, and understand that most people are extrasensory in only one or two ways. If you were extrasensory in every way possible, you'd have a terrible time getting through the day on this earthly plane, as you'd be bombarded nonstop with information!

Extrasensory Training

Use these tips for checking in with your mind and assessing its potential:

- **Close your eyes, clear your mind, and let your senses guide you.** Are you able to "feel" what's in front of you, even though you aren't physically touching it? Can you "see" what's happening in your office, although you aren't there?

- **Learn to focus in on the senses even when you're surrounded by distractions.** The next time you're on a crowded street, see if you can quiet your mind, isolate each sense, and keep moving all at the same time. This will train your senses to stay heightened in any situation.

- **After a week or two of concentrated sense training,** start putting your senses to the test. Begin by making simple predictions. Let's say you're standing in line at the coffee shop. Use your burgeoning power-senses to size up the guy in front of you. What will he order? What will he say to the person serving behind the counter? Will he pay with cash or credit card?

I know these little exercises sound simple, but developing ESP begins with redeveloping the senses in this basic way. Most of us go through the day trying to shut out distractions—sounds, smells, and sights that are superfluous to our immediate concerns. In fact, you need to tune back in to all of that. When you do, you'll be amazed at how obvious some things (like the coffee guy's personality and payment habits) start to seem to you—and how easy it is to predict them.

EXERCISE YOUR WAY TO
SUPER PSYCHIC SKILLS

Once you're a pro at using your perceptions to assess the world around you, you can start using those same skills to predict what's going to happen—using insight to see what the universe holds in store for you.

You might be thinking "Oh, come on—if I could predict the future, I would be rich and nothing bad would ever happen to me or my family!" If only psychic powers worked that way. We are all put into our lives to learn various lessons—and maybe this is just not your time to lead a perfectly charmed life. Wiccans know that there's a definite push and pull in the cosmos, and we're just not meant to see everything before it happens, perhaps especially moments that are meant to teach us something. So don't expect to be receiving all the answers to that important exam you have coming up!

All that said, very skilled psychics can and do see the future. Using your intuition is a necessary step in becoming psychic, and this largely involves sitting back and listening to what your instincts are telling you. But ESP depends on flexing a little mental muscle too. This may sound contradictory, but you need to regularly *work* the right side of your brain—the side that's responsible for creativity and intuition and receptive to psychic messages. It's just like getting stronger anywhere else in your body. If you never lift anything heavier than a can of tuna, you can't expect to have bulging biceps. If you ride in a car all day long, your quadriceps are going to turn to jelly. And if you never work out the creative and visual parts of your brain, they're not going to spit out information when you need it most. Here is a guide to your first "workout."

Meditation Maneuvers

We cannot stress how important it is to take the time to quiet your mind and focus on absolutely nothing. It may sound like a luxury, but when you do this, your mind actually opens up to the very things we're talking about—the things you can't see but can only sense. When you learn to put yourself in a deep state of meditation, so many things become crystal clear. We talk about meditation elsewhere in the book, but it's always attached to another process or activity.

Here are seven steps to help ease you into the "art" of meditation for its own sake:

1. **Make sure you are not so exhausted** that you end up falling asleep. Meditation involves placing yourself in between the sleeping and waking worlds—you don't want to slip over the edge into pure snoozing.

2. **Find a quiet spot without distractions.** Make sure the temperature is comfortable and you have a comfortable place to sit or lie down.

3. **Light some candles, draw the curtains, and play some quiet music.** Binaural tunes, which are recorded in a special way and can induce relaxing brainwaves, are particularly helpful for drawing you into a meditative state. You can easily download this type of music online.

4. **Lie down or sit on the floor or in a chair.** Some people like to meditate cross-legged or in the lotus position, others like to keep their feet flat on the floor. I say assume any position you'll be comfortable in for fifteen to twenty minutes. (If you aren't a yogi, that probably means the lotus position is out.)

5. **Close your eyes. Focus on one sound**—the ticking of the clock, the whir of a fan, the binaural music, the hum of the furnace. Breathe deeply—in through your mouth, out through the nose.

6. **Acknowledge any thoughts that come into your head** and picture putting them in a box for later access. Right now, it's quiet time in the brain.

7. **Now just relax in the nothingness for as long as you can.**

That's really all there is to meditation. It sounds so easy—like, who can't shut off their brain?—but you'd be surprised at how difficult it can be. It's perfectly understandable; we all lead such busy lives, chock-full of appointments, responsibilities, and activities, that it can be tricky to find that quiet place in the mind where the spirit reigns supreme. But that's exactly why we need to do it—so that we don't lose that sense of self.

What does meditation have to do becoming psychic? Most people's brains are so cluttered with day-to-day *stuff* that they can't see the forest for the trees, so to speak. I knew a woman who worked right next to a guy who was absolutely smitten with her. This was obvious to everyone around her, yet she complained that she was invisible to men! She was so harried with work and her outside activities that she couldn't see what was right in front of her. Because of her brain's cluttered condition, there was no way she could have accessed her psychic powers if she needed them. Do I think five to ten minutes of meditation a few times each week could have helped her sort out her love life? I sure do. It would have put her in touch with her intuition, with the world around her, and opened up all kinds of "wormholes" for her to travel down where she could engage her powers of prediction.

See What Your Imagination Can Do

Becoming psychic requires awakening your powers of imagination and visualization as well. This activity is slightly different from meditating, where you want to shut out everything and just *be*. But visualization and imagination exercises start out like meditative workouts, and they go hand in hand.

Find a quiet spot, get into a comfortable position, and close your eyes, just as you would do to begin meditating. This time, though, bring something—an event, a worry, a desire—into your thoughts. Play around with the images, taking them wherever you want. You're controlling the story right now; you can try on different surroundings, different characters, different endings.

You may be asking yourself why you should have to go through all this effort to practice your visualization and imagination, rather than concentrating purely on prediction. Even if your sole aim is prediction (covered in the next chapter), learning to predict events draws on the same part of your brain that holds the imagination, so learning to access and use this region of the mind for visualization strengthens the predictive muscle as well.

SHARPEN YOUR ESP

Not everyone wants to use their psychic skills to perform readings or access other realms of existence; some people just want to know the other planes are there. You can put yourself in environments where there's likely to be a lot of spiritual energy—like old houses and antique stores—but you can also work on this skill in the comfort of your own home.

To sharpen your ESP, you'll need a deck of regular playing cards, a notebook, and a pen. Again, you'll want to create a space that's free of distractions and allows you to concentrate on the task at hand. You may also begin with a meditation if you think this will help open your mind.

Take your deck of playing cards and count out ten red cards and ten black cards. At this point, any suit will do. We just want to focus on the colors.

Shuffle the twenty cards well and place them in a single pile.

In your notebook, write the date and make a two-column chart. Label one column **correct** and the other **incorrect**.

Starting with the first card in the shuffled deck, predict whether it's black or red. Focus your thoughts prior to revealing the card. What is your intuition telling you? Flip over the card. Was your guess correct or incorrect? Tally each prediction in your notebook. Repeat this exercise with each card in the deck. When you finish predicting the colors of every card in the deck, you can easily convert your results to a percentage score. (For example, if you managed to get ten predictions right, your intuition is at 50 percent for this practice.)

Practice this exercise each day. Take special note of how you're feeling on days that you do particularly well or on days when you're particularly off. What affects your intuition? Lack of sleep? Hunger? An argument with someone? A great weekend with your family? Knowing this can let you in on when your psychic abilities are at their best and worst!

As you get better at this skill, you can change the exercise up. For example, split the cards into diamonds and hearts and predict which suit you will pull next. You can make this even more challenging by splitting the cards into four groups of five, organized by suit: five diamonds, five hearts, five spades, and five clubs.

If you feel you've mastered this skill (or you've consistently scored above 50 percent), try shuffling the deck and counting out twenty-six random cards and repeat the exercise. This is very challenging but also a great way to test yourself!

Don't Be a Doubter

Maybe one of the most important aspects of becoming and remaining psychic is to simply *believe* in your abilities. When you waffle, stammer, or constantly second-guess yourself, no vision can come out of such self-doubt. Almost immediately, you will begin to toss your intuition out the window, make poor choices, and lose your faith in the whole process. This is exactly why most people believe they are *not* psychic!

The information is out there, and much of it is yours for the asking (and some of it will come to you even when you don't ask). Accept these gifts as they come to you, use them to do good if and when you can, and learn to enjoy the benefits of experiencing life on as many planes as possible.

Testing Telepathy

We talked about twins being in sync with their thoughts and feelings, but there are many other relationships where this is also true. Mothers can often sense if there is something wrong with their children. Best friends may take on each other's emotions, even on different coasts! There's a simple way to know if you have a truly telepathic relationship with someone: just ask.

Let's say you talk to your sister every Sunday, and you just hung up from a lovely phone call with her. But by Tuesday morning, you're feeling blue for no discernable reason. You just can't figure it out—nothing sad has happened to you and you aren't feeling sick. In fact, everything in your life is going pretty well. Could it be that your sister is the one having an emotionally tough time right now? You can either make a note of it and ask her during your next phone call, or you might want to give her a call and offer your support in the moment you notice.

If you're truly convinced you have a psychic connection with someone, you two can set up experiments to test the validity of your claim. You might both agree to spend $50 on something very general—a pair of pants or a pair of shoes, for instance. Both of you shop on the same day and then compare your goods later that evening. How similar are your choices?

The ultimate telepathic test involves a pack of Zener cards (available online), which feature a series of rudimentary shapes. If you are in the same room as your telepathic connection, one person can look at the cards while the other draws the shape they are sensing. Over the phone, one person can look at the cards and the other can simply state their guess.

Other Ways to Evaluate Your ESP

Some people like the Zener card test; others want to take their abilities out into the world and hone them. There's nothing wrong with that—no matter how you do it, practice makes perfect. Here are some ways to polish your ESP skills daily:

Before you get out of bed in the morning, take a minute to think about your dreams. Was there anything you might decipher as a message, or as an upcoming good or bad event?

While driving to work, what is your sense that you will find a good parking spot? Can you envision it? Does it feel true? Does it happen? If you take public transportation to work, do you have a sense of when your train or bus will arrive? Will you get a seat?

During a conversion, use your skills of observation and heightened senses. What is your sense of the person you're talking with? Are they genuine or phony? What do you think makes this person tick? What is your empathic sense of this person?

Keep track of these experiences—both positive and negative—weekly if not daily. This will give you a real sense of which type of ESP you are strongest in and which may be better left to others. Maybe you will meet someone strong in an area where you are weak, and you can work together to decipher situations and people.

BE YOUR OWN
PSYCHIC THERAPIST

Even if you feel that you don't have one of the ESP traits listed in this chapter, one talent you do have is the psychic ability to read yourself.

How many times have you heard someone say, "If I'd known then what I know now," usually in reference to a choice they made? Sometimes this is a matter of maturity—we make decisions based on a rebellious nature or because we are just too young to appreciate the consequences of our actions. But sometimes we ignore the intuition we're all born with and forge ahead in the wrong direction.

Think about this: more often than not, when things go wrong in a relationship, one of the partners will say, "I should have known. There were so many signs, and I ignored them." After someone has been accused of a terrible crime, people will even say, "There was always something about them that bothered me . . . but I never knew what." Have you shared similar sentiments? That was you tuning into your intuition, knowing something without concrete information.

Thinking about patterns in your life can be especially helpful in this regard. Are there errors you've made over and over again, like poor financial investments or less-than-stellar choices in partner? It is easy to throw your hands in the air and say, "Well, I just make bad decisions!" or "I have the worst luck!" This might be true, but chances are high that a red flag or two showed itself and you turned a blissful, blind eye.

Thankfully, you can open your mind to intuition and learn to use it more successfully.

Start by acknowledging that we all have the skill of intuition.

Learn to quiet your mind as a nightly ritual. This is akin to meditation, but you don't need to go very deep. Just perform a little review of your day—did anything bother you, anything that somehow didn't feel quite right or (on the other hand) felt great?

Take those instances one at a time and explore them. If you had an odd interaction with someone, examine what, exactly, felt different. Some questions to consider:

- **Was it the way in which they spoke to you?**
- **Was there a lack of eye contact?**
- **How did this differ from your usual experience interacting with others?**
- **How did all of this make you feel?**
- **If you felt uncomfortable, what prompted you to feel that way?**
- **Likewise, if you felt unnaturally relaxed (around a boss who normally stresses you out, for example), what made you feel that way?**
- **Most importantly, what do you think was happening with the other person or in the situation?**

Sometimes, you're going to know that something "is up" in a situation, but you won't have the exact answer just yet. That's quite all right. Continue listening to your intuition. Ask the questions you need to ask. Push the issue if you can. Take precautions if possible (like safeguarding your money in a financial relationship or getting yourself away from someone who feels like a threat). The important thing is that your antennae are up now, and you won't be blindsided.

Read the Body Language

If you're interpreting an interaction with another person, then you can also read their subconscious body language to help decipher what's happening.

- **Poor eye contact** means this person is hiding something—either good or bad.

- **Turning away** from you indicates this person is not open to the conversation.

- **Standing right in front of you** or towering over you is an intimidation tactic. Someone might do this to convince you their point of view is truth even when you (and they) know it isn't.

- **Crossing arms or legs** is not necessarily indicative of anything, although some people believe this action shows a person is closed-off and has something to hide. However, someone may just be more comfortable in this position.

- **Enlarged pupils** indicate stress. This is sometimes hard to see, but if you suspect your friend is lying and their pupils are large as life, it's a bad sign for them.

- **Perspiration** is another stress response, indicating anxiety or nervousness.

- **Rapid breathing** is another sign that someone is uncomfortable.

- **People who rock back and forth** or are jittery while seated are anxious about something. The same goes for people who bounce their crossed legs or shake their feet while seated.

- **People will generally back away** from you if they are being dishonest. It's a subconscious move that takes them out of your orbit, so to speak, and allows them to feel less guilty about lying to your face.

- **Someone who touches you while they speak to you** (placing a hand on your arm, for example), really wants you to believe them. It's up to you to read their other body language cues and decide whether they are honest.

Take what you felt in your interaction with someone and couple it with their decoded body language. You will, without a doubt, be on the right track. And don't let anyone tell you differently. We are born with this sense so that we can protect ourselves from danger. If something doesn't feel right, that's all you need to know at that moment. It's very important to not only read body language but trust your gut instinct, especially when it comes to feeling unsafe. If you feel uncomfortable or unsafe in any situation, listen to your instinct and leave. It does not matter if you offend someone—your safety is paramount.

Too often, it's our habit to dismiss out-of-the-ordinary behaviors in someone as them having a bad day. And while we want to give others the benefit of the doubt, we also want to save ourselves from the compounded heartache or headache of knowing something was wrong and failing to act in our own best interest. Women in particular have been socially coded to adhere to principles of politeness—smiling at someone who makes us uncomfortable or being patient and quiet when we clearly want to leave a situation. Do not jeopardize your safety in order to be polite.

Once you hone your ESP, learn to trust your intuition, and make reading into your environment a regular part of your practice, you're going to notice that you make better decisions. This doesn't mean that situations will always turn out the way you want them to, but rather that you don't feel taken advantage of or find yourself on the losing end of matters. Intuition is not quite magick, but it is magickal when used correctly!

Giving A Reading

If you decide to perform readings for the general public, here are a few guidelines to follow:

1. **Keep your meetings to no more than one hour per client.**

2. **Try not to do more than three readings in one day.** Overuse of your psychic ability can often make the readings at the end of the day confusing or muddled, not to mention it will leave you exhausted.

3. **If you are female, never read for a strange man alone in your house.** (Please understand that this means no disrespect to men, but you must safeguard yourself.) It may be a good idea to have someone else in the home if you do read for strangers in general.

4. **Never try to do a reading if you are tired or unwell;** it can often be a waste of everyone's time.

5. **If you are going to charge money for your readings,** keep your fee in line with other clairvoyants or mediums in the vicinity.

6. **If anyone quibbles about paying for a reading,** remind them that they are paying for your time and that this is your chosen profession.

EXTERNAL LINKS
TO THE SIXTH SENSE

While, we are all born with five physical senses and this otherworldly perceptive skill, *all* of our senses are meant to enrich our lives.

For instance, have you ever been in an old house, a historical site, or an antique store and had an uneasy—or very peaceful—feeling come over you? This is a sign that your supersensitive intuition is at work along with your other five senses, letting you know a spirit or some sort of energy is in the area. Those moments are opportunities to tune into your instincts. Even better, they are chances for you to start recognizing whether you can connect through clairvoyance, clairaudience, or other senses.

The next time you find yourself in an environment that seems especially attuned to the afterlife, embrace the opportunity to connect more deeply. Close your eyes and determine what you are experiencing with each of your five senses.

What do you smell? Besides the scents of age, like old books or clothing, do you smell anything more significant?

Is there an odd taste in your mouth?

Are you hearing sounds that can't be explained by the surrounding environment—a voice, laughter, music?

Open your eyes. Do you see anything out of the ordinary? Shadows, streaks of light, mist?

How is your environment affecting your body? Do you have goose bumps? Has there been a sudden drop in temperature?

Also take stock of how you feel internally. Are you queasy? Anxious? Lightheaded?

Strive to open up to that sixth sense now. How do the physical sensations you're experiencing make you feel, emotionally? Are you frightened, curious, or calm?

Checking in with your physical sensations is just as important as paying attention to your sixth sense, so take the time to connect with your body every time you participate in any sort of clairvoyant activity. Visiting historical sites or locations significant to you may be yet another way to sharpen your psychic knack into an area of expertise.

The Psychic In You

People who can naturally sense spiritual energies and entities do have a finely tuned sixth sense, but just because you don't feel your sixth sense now doesn't mean you can't develop it. The biggest lesson you can take from those with psychic abilities is to be open to spiritual encounters. You must welcome the chance to interact on an ethereal level. The more you allow and encourage these occurrences, the more skilled you will become at automatically feeling the truth of a situation and acting on your instincts—psychic or otherwise.

Clairvoyance in any form is not a skill granted to a select few on this earth—with some practice, you can become completely attuned to your psychic abilities, too. Never doubt yourself. If you have a strong feeling about a situation, person, or event, there is most definitely a reason why, so trust your intuitive side and believe in your emotions. Do this and you are halfway there!

Part Two

The Art of Divination

Chapter 3

Scrying:
Crystal Balls
and Mirrors

ALL INTUITIVE PEOPLE HAVE THEIR STRENGTHS AND weaknesses. Some are clairvoyant, while some are scryers. Clairvoyants and scryers tap into the same universal vibrations. It doesn't matter what method you use because the outcome will be the same. If you are a champion image-decipherer (who may say, "Oh, see how that cloud looks like a tree!" or "Wow, that smudge looks like a claw!"), then scrying—also known as crystal gazing, crystal seeing, or peeping— might be *your* thing.

Most scryers use a reflective object like a mirror, crystals, a crystal ball, or even a bowl of water. Some people say that the surface itself serves two purposes: firstly to help draw focus away from the distractions of the surrounding world; and secondly to provide a medium for images to come through.

The image of a wizened old hag slumped over a crystal ball, gazing into the future, is a rather unfortunate visual associated with witches and scrying. While modern-day witches still use a crystal ball for scrying, today's witches are a new breed. We have access to Botox and other "magickal" potions that keep us young and beautiful, so while the typical appearance of a witch has (we hope) changed, what hasn't altered over time is that most witches always have a crystal ball somewhere nearby.

These wonderful objects are not just any old lumps of crystal; they are carefully crafted from the finest materials found on our planet.

THE SKINNY ON SCRYING

Scrying is a way of "seeing" spiritual visions and foretelling the future by looking into a reflective or mutable surface of some kind. Most scryers use a crystal ball or a bowl of water to conjure up their visions, but others use mirrors, crystals, reflective or luminescent stones, or even smoke and fire. It is said that an expert can see visions in something as small and seemingly insignificant as a thumbnail!

Psychic gazing has been a popular practice for centuries, although for different reasons. Some societies used scrying as a means to connect with God, while others understood these visions to be a link to the universe at large. In any event, scrying has survived the test of time and is still practiced today, although it's generally not highly respected among experts in spiritual or scientific fields.

Scrying is such an individual gift that it's impossible to understand or appreciate it unless you can actually *do* it—and if you think you can't scry, then think again. Recent sensory-deprivation studies have given us some insight into how and why visions appear, suggesting that scryers basically shut out distractions from the outside world, allowing their psychic eye to see what no one else sees. In these *ganzfeld* (German for "complete field" or "full field") experiments, participants were deprived of sound and light for a predetermined amount of time. Afterward, participants reported what, if anything, they saw. Months later, many were surprised to discover that their visions had been portents of things to come. The theory is that by blocking out the physical senses, you allow yourself to access areas of the mind that are, too often, ignored and silenced.

Ganzfeld experiments amount to putting yourself into a trance, and you can try this at home without the bells and whistles of a laboratory setting, although you will need a quiet space. Turn off the TV and radio. Put the dog outside. If your apartment or house is subject to the constant din of motorcycles, sirens, and overhead air traffic, turn on a fan for white noise. Now sit comfortably—on the bed, on a chair, at your kitchen table, on the floor, wherever you choose. Choose one spot on the wall in front of you and stare at it. Let your vision go blurry if you want. Breathe deeply

and continue to focus on that one spot. Within a couple of minutes, the spot will begin to darken, suggesting that your sense of sight has had enough. You can continue on at this point—what can you "see" in your mind's eye?—or simply move your eyes to another area of the room to bring yourself, and your senses, back.

I See the History of Scrying

In ancient Egypt, priests and priestesses used scrying as a way to divine the future. They would pour oil or water into a dark vessel and wait for images to appear, using the results to predict the outcome of war, the best time to plant crops, or the best time to conceive a child. The images would be dark and fuzzy, but that didn't really matter. It was their *interpretation* of the images that was important.

Some people used scrying as a form of meditation to get in touch with their spiritual sides. Other seers, perhaps because of the changes in the alpha waves in their brains, were able to enter into hypnotic states, or self-induced trances, in which they predicted future events.

As the centuries rolled on, the art of scrying evolved. Surfaces included water, knife blades, pools of ink, ice, and even fingernails that had been buffed to a shine—all of which were accessible to the ordinary person. Crystal balls were another story—they were expensive and used only by wealthy families.

At that time, people believed that crystals were permanently frozen water and, as such, were infused with magick. Well, they were on the right track— even though crystals are not representative of a deep freeze, they are, of course, magick in the palm of your hand!

The ancient Druids were thought to be the first users of crystal balls, which were tiny by today's standards, measuring about ½ inch (1 cm) in diameter, and made from obsidian, beryl, aquamarine, and chrysoberyl. Crystal gazers often scryed in a dim room, but sometimes they took the crystal outside, held it up to the sunlight, and gazed upon it while looking toward the sky. As you might expect, this resulted in scryers reporting problems with their eyesight, and so the practice was quickly abandoned.

During the time of the Druids, crystal ball gazing was often used in magickal ceremonies and to reveal the secrets of the past. This included the purification and blessing of the sphere by a magician who would anoint it with a unique blend of olive oil. Typically, a young boy (a representation of purity of mind) was called upon to do the scrying, and he would report seeing a spirit in the ball if the reading was a success.

Some scholars believe that Nostradamus used scrying as a method of divination. It is said that he would often stare into a bowl of water to bring on this special state of consciousness when writing his famous quatrains predicting future wars, deaths, and world calamities.

It wasn't until the Victorian age that the Roma people, with their dark, flowing hair and vibrant sense of style and dress, brought attention back to the crystal ball. The Roma were well versed in this divinatory art.

Though they were much maligned during this period, the Roma were also known to be very good at scrying. In fact, they elevated this mystical science to an art form. Their fortune-telling abilities were so revered that when people living in towns and cities saw the wagons coming, they scraped some money together and scurried to have their fortunes read before the Roma hit the road again!

Crystal Enhancement

In those Victorian times, witches, warlocks, and wizards began taking this ancient form of crystal gazing to an even higher level of development and skill. They refined the technique of scrying by choosing crystals with specific properties attached to them and using those crystals for divination, healing, and enlightenment. If a client had a fertility problem, for example, she would hold a crystal or crystals in her hand— usually moonstone and/or rose quartz—while the witch gazed into the scrying surface. The crystal would wipe out the negative forces surrounding the person, opening the door to peace and contentment.

Lapis lazuli was, and still is, often used to help people find inner peace, while rose quartz brought love and self-healing. There are so many stones out there it could boggle the mind, so use the simple list below as a starting

guide (and see chapter 4, "Crystal Divination," for more information on crystals):

- **AMETHYST:** Higher consciousness
- **BLUE AGATE:** Inner consciousness
- **CITRINE:** Money and success
- **HEMATITE:** Opportunity
- **QUARTZ:** Clarity of mind
- **SAPPHIRE:** Truth
- **MALACHITE:** Past lives

To boost the power of the vision, choose a crystal that relates to the reason you're scrying.

CONNECTING WITH THE CRYSTAL BALL

If you want to give a crystal ball a whirl, try to stop in at a New Age shop. You can buy a crystal ball on the Internet, too, but because I believe that you have to be drawn to a crystal, I really recommend that you try to purchase one in person so you can choose the one that "speaks" or "calls" to you. It's a lot easier to determine a good match if you can pick it up, hold it, feel its vibrations, and connect with it. Stand back, look at the array of balls available in the shop, and see what looks appealing to you. A certain color? A specific material? Hold each ball that you like and just close your eyes for a moment. Does the ball have an energy that you can feel? Does the weight feel right to you? Are you happy holding it?

These days, most crystal balls are usually made of quartz, and experts in crystallomancy recommend using one that has at least a 2½-inch (6 cm) diameter, so that any images that appear are easier to see. If you're shopping for a ball this size, you should be aware of two things:

1. **They can be quite expensive.**

2. **They usually include imperfections called veils,** which are normal and will not affect your ability to see images during a scrying session.

Many scrying balls advertised as crystal are actually glass. While it's fine to use a glass ball, a ball made of glass are (or should be) a fraction of the price. You can tell if a ball is made of glass because it will have no imperfections. Zero. Crystal, on the other hand, always has some sort of defects—smudges, flecks, or bubbles inside the crystal—which is anything but detrimental to its power in revealing the secrets of the universe. Imperfections are not necessarily a bad thing; in fact, they may well help you with your visions. Again, this is a purely personal matter. Some scryers can live with a couple of tiny flaws and others are distracted by them, so you should go with what feels right to you.

A real crystal ball that fits into the palm of your hand can easily cost $50 or more. A glass ball, meanwhile, might cost about a third of that.

Purists say that there is simply no substitute for crystal when scrying. They say it's more powerful and gives better results. It's believed that some crystal balls will know when the right potential owner holds it in their hands and will work to make the connection happen. That is, the ball will speak to the right person and make itself available at the right time for the right price.

Our advice is to try a glass ball if you can't afford the real deal. You could even scatter some of smaller crystals around the table as a means of boosting the glass's energy. There are no guarantees on the results you'll get, but it never hurts to combine spiritual forces in this way.

Whenever you see a movie with a crystal gazer, the person will inevitably have a giant sphere placed on a stand in front of them. In real life, the ball is smaller and can be held on a piece of black velvet in the scryer's hands. (If you do have a stand for your crystal ball, make sure you place the stand itself on top of a piece of black velvet during your reading.)

Preparing and Storing Your Crystal Ball

Before using your crystal ball, you'll need to cleanse it. Choose one of these four methods:

1. **Place a new washcloth or dishtowel** in the bottom of your sink. Place your ball on top and run warm water over it. Imagine any negative energy being washed away in this gentle bath.

2. **Put your crystal ball in a bowl of salt overnight.** The salt will absorb dark energy. Make sure to discard the salt afterward.
   [**Note:** *Make sure it is not a type of crystal that dissolves in water or is eroded by salt! See page 89 for more on this.*]

3. **Hold the ball in your hand** and waft sage incense all around it.

4. **Leave it out under a full moon** for the night.

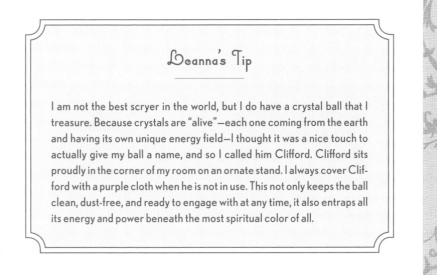

You should cleanse your crystal ball once a month. Allow twenty-four hours between scrying sessions. To recharge your crystal ball between sessions, place it in the moonlight overnight.

Whatever their size, crystal balls are typically mounted on a stand so they don't roll away. A small pillow or pad will do, although some balls come with their own little stands. When the ball is not in use, it is always best to cover it with a piece of white, gold, or purple velvet.

Deanna's Tip

I am not the best scryer in the world, but I do have a crystal ball that I treasure. Because crystals are "alive"—each one coming from the earth and having its own unique energy field—I thought it was a nice touch to actually give my ball a name, and so I called him Clifford. Clifford sits proudly in the corner of my room on an ornate stand. I always cover Clifford with a purple cloth when he is not in use. This not only keeps the ball clean, dust-free, and ready to engage with at any time, it also entraps all its energy and power beneath the most spiritual color of all.

A SUCCESSFUL SCRY

Scrying is best done at night, ideally during the full moon or the nights leading up to it (aka the waxing moon phase), though some scryers gaze whenever the mood strikes them. *All* these methods are subject to modification, so you should do whatever you find works best for you.

Prepare a quiet space for yourself that is free of distractions. Make this space as open to the spirit world and the universe as possible. Create a soothing and relaxing atmosphere that will encourage the universe to work with you.

Turn off your phone. If you find music helpful, play it on a low volume. Set your crystal ball on its stand or pillow on a table, or if you are using another reflective surface, place it on a sturdy workspace. Make sure it's at a height where you can look into it comfortably from wherever you are seated. Have a notebook and pen nearby to record your observations once your session ends. Light a white candle and place it near the scrying surface. You can also burn incense or scatter crystals of your choosing around the workspace.

The key to successful scrying is one part focus and one part relaxation. Open your eyes now and look into your ball or surface, but keep that unfocused state going. To see the future, you don't have to ask anything. You may see a cloud taking shape in the ball; you may see visions. You're not trying to see anything specific, so just accept whatever it is that appears and don't try to rush it.

The ball is a good source of information concerning the past, present, or future, so you can also ask it virtually anything. Remember, this is your divination work and you can seek whatever you want. There are no limits. Maybe you want to know if you're going to find a suitable partner in the next year. Or perhaps you'd like to know if you're going to get promoted at work. Then again, you may want to know if you'll be coming into a significant amount of money that is unrelated to work.

Once you have the question in mind, you want to let your mind soften and even blur as much as possible—this is the relaxation. Close your eyes. Take several deep breaths, inviting quiet and stillness into your mind. Open your heart to the universe. Allow everything else to fall away.

Now open your eyes and turn your gaze toward your scrying surface. Let your vision unfocus and even go blurry. If you feel yourself slipping into something like a trance, that's okay—go with it. Breathe deeply and know that you will see images related to your question.

Focus on your question and look at your surface. What do you see? Some of the images may not make sense at first, and that's okay. When you are done, you will have time to decipher what you have seen. For now, just allow the images to appear for as long as they keep coming to you.

When the images slow or stop, bring yourself back to full consciousness and start writing about what you observed. No matter how odd or irrelevant it may seem, jot it down. It may be that some of the information is cloudy and confusing right now, but as the days go on, it will become more important to you.

Here's what you can expect during a successful session:

1. **A cloud will appear in the center of the ball,** indicating that spiritual energy is taking hold. It is usually white, but it may change colors.

2. **The cloud will eventually fade to darker gray or black.**

3. **Images related to a query might appear next and in quick succession.** Don't be alarmed—just take it all in.

4. **The images will eventually fade into a mist before disappearing.**

Once the fog has dissipated, wrap your crystal ball in the velvet cloth and set it aside. Now, in your Book of Shadows or journal, write down what you saw in the ball, whether or not it makes sense.

Friends may want you to peer into your scrying surface with their concerns in mind, as well. If you conduct a scrying session for another person, it helps to have an idea of what they want to know, just as you would do for yourself. This is easier than attempting to see the vast, general future. This makes sense: the universe holds an infinite amount of information, so you may get bits and pieces regarding different areas of a person's future, and these may, in turn, be difficult to put together into a cohesive reading.

MIRROR DIVINATION

Mirrors are frequently featured in fairy tales and mystical stories, often representing a veil between two worlds or a device that grants its owner magickal abilities. Think of Snow White's evil stepmother, the Queen, asking, "Who's the fairest of them all?" The mirror not only told her that Snow White was still alive; it also said Snow White was more even more beautiful that the Queen herself. Another example can be found in *Alice's Adventures in Wonderland*, where a young girl steps through a mirror to a fantastical world. Everything Alice experienced was just on the other side of that reflective surface, alive and well the whole time. In yet another example, in stories about the wizard Merlin of Arthurian legend, he is often said to possess a magickal mirror that let him see anywhere in the realm.

A mirror can also capture our souls—or lack thereof. In lore, vampires have no reflection, and some cultures reject the use of mirrors because of a belief that it may alter or damage the soul. Breaking a mirror is supposed to cause you seven years' bad luck, but why? This probably has to do with the belief that our souls can be contained in a mirror's reflection, and breaking the mirror causes the soul to scatter somewhat.

When Jews practice the seven-day mourning ritual of sitting shiva, mirrors in the home are covered. One reason for this is to reflect on grief without focusing on one's physical appearance. Kabbalists, however, believe that a time of grief is ripe for the dark energies of anger, regret, and guilt to enter a home through a mirror's surface.

Mirrors also show us the absolute reality of our world—or at least what is visible to the naked eye. In this book we focus more on what *isn't* readily apparent to us. That's where our crystal mirror divination comes in.

Black Obsidian Mirror Scrying

The magickal black mirror is the gold standard for mirror scrying. These mirrors are usually constructed from black obsidian. They are prepared for use with a special cleansing ritual before being fused together and rubbed with an herbal blend that attracts and holds the highest amount of spiritual energy.

To charge your mirror, you must leave it outside to bathe under the light of a full moon. City dwellers can leave the mirror on a windowsill. The window should be left open, either fully or partly, depending on the weather.

Place a moonstone and something made from gold on the surface; this helps to really empower the mirror. (Remember that the moonstone is noted for its qualities of intuition, magick, mysticism, dream activation, lucid dreaming, serenity, positive insight, and protection.)

The black scrying mirror has many uses in the world of magick, including:

- **Connection to spirit guides.**
- **Augmenting wisdom and knowledge** (aka deepening your connection to the spiritual and seeking more profound connections and knowing).
- **Access to Akashic records,** a collection of all thoughts, emotions, intentions, knowing, words, prayers, and actions that have ever or will ever occur, according to the nineteenth-century

Russian occultist Helena Blavatsky. They exist on an etheric plane and are accessible only through spiritual connection.

- **Astral projection and travel,** or the manner of one's spirit leaving the body and experiencing other dimensions, realms, and spiritual planes.

- **Divination of the future.**

- **Self-healing and meditation.**

- **Transmission of information to spiritual realms.**

Although your black mirror can be used at any time, regular scryers say that their mirrors—not unlike other magickal tools—tend to work best during a full moon. You don't have to worry too much, though; you can use your mirror during any moon phase—it will still work. Magickal mirrors are used quite differently from the average looking glass. For one, they're used in the dark. Many black mirrors come with stands, but you can also place the mirror on a flat surface or in the palm of your hand for scrying. You can light a candle and place the mirror to the side of the mirror or behind it (if your mirror is on a stand), or in the moonlight, as discussed previously. You want your mirror's surface to be a blank, dark canvas, as though you are looking into a tunnel or portal.

Make sure the mirror's surface is clean. You can wipe it with a soft cloth and a little rubbing alcohol to remove smudges. Although you aren't using the mirror to see in the most literal sense, you don't want anything on its surface to distract you.

Place your mirror in its intended place, making sure it's stable and visible to you. This sounds obvious, but again, once you are engaged in this process, you don't want anything to break your focus. Don't, for example, lean a large mirror on an object that may fall midway through your session.

To prepare for this ritual, first take a cleansing shower or bath. You should also prepare your space ahead of time so that it's ready to go when you are. You can incorporate the black mirror into a crystal grid (see pages 95–96), or you can use it by itself. Now let's begin scrying:

1. **Close your eyes and imagine both you and the mirror in a protective white light.** The light swirls and encircles you from top to bottom. Maybe it shimmers; maybe there is a star included in its beams. Allow the light to enter your chakras, from top to bottom, infusing your being with harmony and peace.

2. **Place your hands at the sides of your mirror and let that light transfer into it.** You may move your hands up and down the edges of the mirror, but avoid touching the surface. When you feel the charge is complete, bring the light back to your own being.

3. **Now close your eyes and breathe deeply.** Concentrate on any tense areas in your body, like your neck, your back, or your shoulders. Feel your ribs expand with each inhalation and imagine your lungs deflating fully during your exhalation. Continue to do this until you feel you are fully relaxed and able to engage with the spiritual plane. The goal is to put yourself into a light trance.

4. **Repeat your intention to yourself, being as specific as you can.** This is a good time to connect with a spirit or the universe, to appeal for guidance. You can call on your guides with a simple incantation, something like *"I ask {spirit} to guide me toward the answers I am seeking. I ask that you help visions come to me unhindered and completely."*

5. **With your question in mind, open your eyes and gaze into the mirror, using it as a focal point for the visions coming to mind.** This is kind of like focused daydreaming—the difference being that you are aware of the images coming to your mind. Let the visions wander where they will—you do not need to have control over them, nor should you try to direct them. This can be difficult for someone who likes to be in charge, but right now, a spirit is sending the signals—so sit back and just receive.

6. **When you feel that the apparitions are slowing or have come to a clear conclusion, close your eyes again.** Stretch your neck to the left, right, front, and back, and slowly bring yourself back to full alertness. Give gratitude to your spirit guides for what you've seen and experienced.

7. **Reach for your journal or Book of Shadows and pen and write down what you've experienced.** Put everything on the page, even if it doesn't make sense to you right now. Confusing images might take on a new meaning during any future scrying sessions or during your daily interactions.

It may be tempting to dive into a black mirror divination daily, especially if you currently have a major life issue around which you're seeking clarity. However, make sure you give yourself enough time between sessions to process your visions. You don't want to end up confusing or overwhelming yourself!

IT'S MY TV AND
I'LL SCRY IF I WANT TO

A few years ago, I [Shawn] was sitting daydreaming and my eyes inadvertently drifted over toward my television, which was turned off at the time. I began to see the same kinds of visions on the blank screen that I usually see in my crystal ball. This probably happened because I was in an almost trancelike state and my mind was clear of distractions. Later, I decided to experiment: I turned the television on, but instead of setting it to a particular channel, I simply unscrewed the cable connector and turned the TV to a blank screen with white noise and "snow." White noise is commonly used to connect with ghosts and spirits who are looking to communicate with the living, so I got to thinking, "Why not use it in scrying? Maybe someone out there has something to share with me through white noise." And you know what? I was amazed at the results! In some respects, the visions I encountered were much clearer than the methods of scrying I had tried in the past.

Since you may not have a crystal ball, this method is a great way to try out the skill of scrying without investing in an expensive tool. This is a brand-new divinatory art called "plasma scrying." It's quite simple, and you don't have to pay the cable company for an extra channel on your television set. It's free, courtesy of the Twilight Zone!

The first step in successful plasma scrying is to make sure your television set is either turned off or set to a blank channel. [**Note:** if you have a smart TV and/or a fiber-optic connection, try finding a white-noise static channel on YouTube that you can play on your television screen instead. Or, try a laptop or cell—see bottom of page and page 80. Do not clean the screen. Any smudges or specks will add to your visions, not detract from them. The next important steps are:

1. **Do not shut off all the lights in the room** or you won't be able to see any reflection on the television screen. In addition to whatever lighting you have in the room, you will also need a white candle. I like to use a small white candle in a glass.

2. **Start by saying this incantation:** *"To the technology born, I give it light, to show me the way, to my own inner light. So mote it be."* Write this down in your Book of Shadows for future reference.

3. **Now, light the white candle** and place it in front of the television set or laptop. Make sure the candlelight casts a flickering glow or light on the screen.

4. **Stare at the blank screen** and begin daydreaming.

5. **In your mind, ask a question** about anything that is important to you: partner, job, career, or family. Within about ten minutes the answer should be revealed.

Smaller Scryers

If the TV screen does not work for you or you are not near a TV, take out your laptop computer and open it, but don't turn it on. Place it on your lap. Repeat all the above steps, but omit the lit candle to avoid setting yourself or your computer on fire.

Or, take out your smartphone or tablet. Stare at the reflection on the screen for five minutes. (Again, forget lighting a candle. You have enough problems at the moment trying to conjure up an image.) I'll bet my witch's cap you will see something. Why? It's like learning anything else. Sometimes, to see, you have to start small, and a tiny screen can help you focus more quickly and more clearly.

Some people think that when they stare at their screens, they will see a live "show" of the future. That's not really what we're trying to do, but if this exercise inspires you to write a script or a proposal, then by all means, go for it.

Successful screen scrying isn't like watching a show; it's all in the interpretation of the dust spots, smudges, fingerprints, and reflections of light on the screen. It is up to you to mentally process those shapes and forms and discover how they relate to you. This is the same principle as cloud-watching and can be applied anytime, anywhere.

READING THE RESULTS

Remember when you were a kid gazing at the clouds in the sky and you swore they looked liked dragons, or faces, or rocket ships, or other imaginary shapes in your mind? Some of the images were scary, some were comforting, others were just there. Use that same skill to associate an image with the flickering lights on the television screen or in your crystal ball. Does the image look dark and scary or happy or warm? What feelings do you get from the image?

This is where a trancelike state of mind comes into play. To interpret what you're seeing, you have to get off the mental plane and into a zoned-out state where those images can come to life. People sometimes ask me

how to "read" what they're seeing, as though there are right, wrong, or definite answers in the world of scrying. Whatever you see will be related to your own experiences or, if you're reading for someone else, connected to something happening in that person's life. Let's say you conjure up a vision of a harp—and your grandfather happened to be a harpist. Perhaps the message coming through is from him or about him. If a vision is difficult to see or appears to be very small, it probably means that it's either a past event or something that will happen in the distant future. Strong, clear visions indicate something that is imminent.

Colors in your visions can also indicate what's to come:

- **WHITE:** Protection, positive energy
- **RED:** Danger
- **ORANGE:** Anger
- **YELLOW:** Trouble, obstacles ahead
- **BLUE:** Success
- **GREEN:** Happiness, health
- **BLACK, GRAY:** Negative energy

Each person has their own divinatory ability that is unique only to them. But in order to succeed at this art, you have to try each and every one of the methods to find the one that you are most comfortable with and enjoy the most.

Chapter 4

Crystal Divination

CRYSTALS ARE USED AND TREASURED BY ALMOST every culture, religion, and society. For centuries, royals all over the world have donned priceless studded crowns that have been coveted. Crystals have been incorporated into glamorous jewelry and used as healing or magickal talismans. They have been celebrated, fought over, and displayed with pride. We mine crystals, revere them for their beauty, and even use them in modern technology. They contain the planet's DNA, stamped with millions of years of evolutionary history.

Why is it that even today, we regard these cherished gemstones with such intensity, and why is it that we carry on these time-honored fascinations? It is probably because crystals embody magick. These captivating, enchanting stones carry so much mysticism that even today, we can't fully understand the extent of their power.

CRYSTALS FOR DIVINATION AND PSYCHIC AWARENESS

Even if you've been divining for years, you can always add something unique by using certain stones to enhance your practice.

Following are a range of crystals to use with divination. The best s tones to have on hand are starred with an asterisk, but you may find that there is one stone you genuinely feel a strong connection with, so if this is the case, go ahead and incorporate it into your session!

You also may want to keep a journal of your observations and make note of which crystals you have used in your Book of Shadows.

AGATE Protects and soothes, promotes confidence

AGATE (Holly blue) Helps unleash psychic abilities; manifests a spiritual intention

AMETHYST Useful for opening the third eye chakra and expanding one's psychic abilities

ALBITE For any kind of spiritual work; boosts psychic powers

AMBLYGONITE Unlocks psychic energy, releases stress, and helps one break away from emotional ties

APATITE (blue) Enhances insight and psychic abilities

APOPHYLLITE (clear) Heals emotional wounds and helps recovery from past events; opens the soul to other spiritual and psychic planes

ARAGONITE (blue) Good for working with divination, as it brings perception and insight and helps psychic connections

AZEZTULITE™ (red fire) Recently discovered in the United States, part of the quartz family; a powerful shielding stone said to keep one safe; for connection with solar gods and power; use in any spells that call for protection; improves vigor, wisdom, passion, endurance, and psychic/visualization abilities

AZURITE Also works with the third eye and throat chakras to promote clairvoyance, insight, and psychic vision.

BENITOITE For psychic enhancement and channeling of energies; heightens intuition; can be used in healing, especially in directing good energy toward those with blood disorders

BERYL Gives strength when dealing with stress and also removes emotional baggage; used also to boost scrying techniques; an overall good healing stone; many colors and varieties (including aquamarine, emerald, goshenite, heliodor, morganite)

BLOODSTONE Expands clairvoyance and encourages lucid dreaming

CALCITE Promotes astral travel and journeying to other realms

CAVANSITE Develops and enhances psychic abilities and spiritual perception; allows one the freedom to change their mindset

CHRYSOBERYL For enhancement of psychic dreams and vision and protection from evil and the evil eye; inspires forgiveness; use this crystal for self-control, especially when trying to lose weight; also effective for any kind of learning or studying

COVELLITE (Covelline) Assists with psychic development, spiritual awakening, insight, perception, and connection to a higher spiritual plane

DUMORTIERITE For focus, intellectual enhancement, motivation and creativity, and psychic visions

FLUORITE Works with the third eye to bring clarification to psychic visions

HACKMANITE (blue) A cleansing stone; can be used to eliminate negative energies and improve psychic ability

HALITE (blue) Promotes happiness and feelings of well-being; also used for enhancing mindfulness and psychic awareness

IOLITE Enhances all forms of supernatural powers

JEREMEJEVITE Rare; for any kind of divination

KYANITE Often used in wand formation; increases the powers of perception, intuition, and channeling spiritual styles and messages

LABRADORITE One of the workhorse crystals; collaborates with one's highest energy and enhances every psychic skill

LAPIS LAZULI Used for protection from dark forces while channeling psychic power; opens the third eye to enhance psychic visions

MOLDAVITE Powerful, and extraterrestrial; increases psychic abilities; removes blocks and obstacles

MOONSTONE Works best during the full moon, to expand intuition; useful when scrying with black mirrors

MUSCOVITE Improves psychic abilities and boosts mental power; effective in spells for improving intellect

OBSIDIAN Enhances one's connection to the spirit world during scrying and improves psychic vision

PHENAKITE For psychic vision, inner awakenings, third eye stimulation, and astral travel

PROPHECY STONE (limonite and hematite pseudomorph) Furthers psychic vision

QUARTZ Enhances the highest form of energy and protects against dark forces; thought to be the most powerful amplifying stone, giving all stones in its vicinity a lift

QUARTZ (Tanzan aura) Amplifies insight, wisdom, and psychic vision

TITANIUM For peace, harmony, abundance, and amplification of positive energy; raises the spiritual energies; good to use alongside divination

RHODIZITE Amplifies power of other crystals; enhances psychic abilities and emotional strength

RUBY KYANITE Boosts cash flow and psychic awareness

SAPPHIRE All colors can be used to expand intuition, astral travel, and third eye vision

SODALITE Removes sluggishness; for opening one's deepest thoughts and desires, perception, intellect, and prophetic vision; improves perception and understanding of psychic messages

TEKTITE Thought to open one up to telepathic communication and a link with otherworldly energies and beings

TIFFANY STONE (Purple Passion) May give one's sex life a helping hand; helps its user grow psychically

TOPAZ (blue) Boosts psychic ability, spiritual growth, and spiritual communication

TURQUOISE Enhances communication between its user and their spirit guides/universal forces

ULEXITE Amplifies visualization and improves psychic abilities

POSITIONING AROUND THE HOME

Crystals do not just project power; they also act like sponges and absorb the energy around them. With this in mind, it's important to consider where in the home you'll store your crystals. If you opt to store your magickal stones out on display in this way, consider that the crystal's energy could become contaminated. Visitors might casually pick them up, transfer their energy onto your crystals, and they will need to be cleansed before their next use.

The preferred placement and storage of a crystal can also change depending on the variety. For example, placing amethyst or citrine on a windowsill is not a good idea, as these varieties are highly pigmented and will fade if exposed to sunlight. For smaller tumbled stones, try craft boxes with individual compartments. A small label positioned inside each compartment can also be helpful for reminding yourself what each stone is called and what spells it might be used for. (You can also keep such notes in your Book of Shadows.)

Some witches like to wrap larger crystals in red cloth. This color has the slowest rate of energy absorption, so it acts as an energy barrier. Just be sure that the fabric has natural fibers; crystals do not respond well to synthetic materials.

If you have more than one kind of stone, try to separate them according to their variety. This way the energy of one stone won't spill into the crystal sitting next door to it.

CRYSTAL CLEANSING AND CHARGING

While crystals can attract positive energy, they can also hold on to negative energy. Crystals that are used in clearing negative energy should be cleansed before being used again. You might notice that after such a ritual, your crystal will feel hot or heavy, or look particularly lackluster. You're not imagining things; the stone is just doing its job and removing unwanted energy from a chakra or aura. If you have a crystal you've been relying on for some time and it seems to have lost its *oomph*, you should think about giving it a reasonable cleanse and recharge. A regular crystal cleansing will not only recharge your gems; it will rid them of all invisible debris. Some people like to purify regularly and perform a cleansing once a month. For magickal uses, it is always best to cleanse your crystals before and after any ritual. There are multiple ways to do this, so here we have listed a few to get you started.

Smudging with Sage

Sage bundles act as a spiritual disinfectant. They can be purchased from any New Age store or online. Using a lighter or match, carefully light the end of the sage bundle in a safe area—outside or in a nonflammable area. Let it burn for a few moments, then blow out the flames. (Please exercise caution; your sage bundle should *never* be completely

engulfed in flames.) With your crystal in one hand and the sage bundle in the other, waft the crystal through the smoke for about thirty seconds. This is a quick and efficient method of purification; it's one of the most common methods used by witches today.

Freshwater Bath

Submerging your stones in water from a running stream, spring, pond, or lake is a natural and effective method of cleansing. Be aware, though, that you cannot use this method with some crystals. Celenite can dissolve, and hematite will rust when left in water too long. For stones with sensitivity to liquids, the smudging technique is a safer bet.

Saltwater Bath

You can cleanse many crystals with a saltwater rinse or bath. Just fill a glass or ceramic bowl with salt water—a palmful of sea salt should suffice for a quart of water, and less salt for less water—and place your crystal(s) in it. You can allow it to soak for as little as one hour, but if you think your crystal has been loaded down with a particularly heavy energy, you can leave it in to soak for up to one week. When your cleanse is complete, rinse your stone in cool spring water and toss the salt bath away.

Note that some stones can be damaged by salt—generally anything that's porous (like opal) or has high water content. Pyrite, hematite, and lapis lazuli should not be soaked in salt water. For these stones, it is best to use the smudging technique.

If you're lucky enough to have a large, crystal-holding geode with a cavity, you can use it cleanse other crystals very successfully. Geodes are known for their ability to neutralize negative energy and replace it with positive vibes. Crystals should be placed inside of the geode cavity for at least twenty-four hours.

Sea Salt

Pure sea salt can be purchased from any local store and is a good way to rid your crystal of imperfect vibes. Pour the salt into a large-enough bowl, making sure that the crystals are completely covered. Don't touch them for a few hours. You can also substitute earth, clay, or sand for salt. Always dispose of the salt you've used for cleansing—don't reuse it for another cleanse. It contains the negative energy it has drawn out of the crystal. (See page 89 though for a note about certain stones that should not be used with salt.)

Sunlight and Moonlight

Light from the sun and the moon not only cleanses your crystals—it also can be used to give them a recharge. Placing your stones outside during the day or overnight to soak in the rays will provide them with a boost. You can lay them on the ground, on an outside table, or on a windowsill. It's recommended, no matter whether you cleanse during the day or during the night, that you do so during a full moon phase, as it's a time when magickal happenings take place.

However, if you really can't wait for the full moon to arrive, make sure that, whatever the phase, the sun or the moon is at least visible in the sky. To revitalize your crystals during the daytime, leave them outside when the sun is at its brightest. This is a quick cleanse that only takes a few hours, but again, make sure that light-sensitive crystals such as citrine and amethyst are not left in the heat of the sun for more than thirty minutes—they will fade.

Tibetan Bells

The sound from the chimes of Tibetan bells retunes crystals and gives them a healing boost. Place the stones on a flat surface and gently ring the bells over the top of them repeatedly.

EMPOWERING YOUR CRYSTAL

The following is relevant information and must be understood before any ritual takes place.

When empowering your stones or crystals, make sure that you spend at least five minutes beforehand holding the stone and envisaging the desired result of your spell in your mind's eye. When you do this, you are making a personal connection with it so that it recognizes your energy and will work its magick alongside you.

Because crystals absorb energies and emotions, the crystal you plan to use will work better if it knows exactly what you want it to do. If you have trouble visualizing, speak to your stone out loud and express your wish to it.

The preparation and methods for the spells in this book will vary, so be sure to read the entire spell thoroughly before commencing. Follow each direction to the letter.

Candles

If your spell calls for the use of candles, then, unless otherwise stated, these must be left to burn down on their own (always supervised, of

course). If you blow them out prematurely, your ritual may not be as successful. Tealight or votive candles are well suited for this purpose. Please be vigilant when you light the candles and make sure that they are properly adhered to a suitable holder. Never leave a candle unattended or within reach of small children. Sometimes a spell will take place over the span of a couple of days. In these cases, the candle may be extinguished and relit later.

Closing the Ritual

Whenever you cast a spell, no matter its source, in many cases, it's a standard tradition that you repeat a chant or mantra. The number of times you recite the incantation varies from spell to spell, but it is essential that once you have spoken the ritual in full, you close it down by saying the words *"So mote it be."*

"Topping Up" Your Stone

When a crystal is present during a spell, it soaks in the ritual's aura and effects. If you use a crystal in a spell with long-term intentions, don't cleanse it after the spell. Instead, allow the crystal to radiate this power— it should last for at least two months. If the effects of your spell seem to begin waning after that time, and you need the spell to continue, the crystal may need to be "topped up." Go ahead and perform the spell a second time. Once a spell has worked and your final desired solution has been attained, then go ahead and cleanse.

A Spell for Strengthening Psychic Abilities

As with anything, the more you rehearse any type of divination, the better you will become, but you can boost your ability from time to time, making your readings or predictions more successful.

There are quite a few crystals we can use for this purpose, but the best by far is albite. This crystal can be pricey, though, so if it is outside your budget, you might want to choose another from the list on pages 83–87.

Materials

An albite or corresponding crystal, to boost psychic awareness

A large tall tapered or block candle, in white

A glass bowl

Spring water or rainwater, enough to fill the bowl

Ritual

Cleanse and empower your crystal (see pages 88–92). On the night of a waning moon, sit in a comfortable chair and empower your crystal by holding it on your forehead chakra for about ten minutes. During this time, concentrate on the power of the stone and imagine that it is projecting psychic rays directly into your brain.

Stand in front of your altar and place a lit white candle, to symbolize purity, and a glass bowl filled with the water in the center. Drop the crystal into the bowl, turn off the lights, and gaze into the water for a few minutes. When the water is still, dip your finger into the bowl to create a ripple and then dab your wet finger on your forehead. Say the following spell nine times:

> *"Psychic powers rise within me,*
> *increase my awareness, let me see,*
> *Fill my being with glorious light,*
> *when the moon wanes on this magickal night."*

After you've recited the spell nine times, close it by adding *"So mote it be."* Blow out the candle. Repeat the water-dabbing ritual and relight the candle before you conduct any psychic work or divination.

A Spell for Heightening Your Instincts

We're big advocates for trusting your instincts, but like most people, there are times when we reject our intuitions and live to regret it afterward. It is so important that you listen to your soul. If something doesn't feel right, or you get a creepy feeling about a person, this is an instinctive warning bell and you must take notice!

Materials

A benitoite crystal

1 whole lemon, to improve concentration

1 bay leaf, to stimulate intuition

A bowl

A votive or tealight candle, in yellow

Spring water or rainwater, enough to fill the bowl

Cotton balls

Ritual

Cleanse and empower your crystal (see pages 88–92). On a full moon, slice the whole lemon in half and place it, along with the bay leaf and crystal, in the bowl. Set this on your altar. Light the candle next to the bowl and recite the following spell three times:

> *"I perceive my truth, my inner voice,*
> *the facts I heed I won't misread."*

After you've recited the spell three times, close it by adding *"So mote it be."* While the candle is burning, pour the water into the bowl and allow everything to steep until the candle has burned down. Drain just the water into a clean container and put it in the fridge. Every day, drench a cotton ball with the magickal water and place it against the center of your forehead for a few seconds. This potion should last for at least a month.

CRYSTAL GRIDS

Like intuition, psychic powers are something many of us are born with, but we learn to dismiss them during our formative years. This is a shame, of course, because we lose our connection to an entire universe filled with so much information. Think about how happy we would all be if we were completely confident in our thoughts and actions.

The good news is that there are many ways to regain your innate psychic abilities. One of the best methods is to use a crystal grid.

The use of specific crystal layouts dates back thousands of years. Many of the shapes used are based on sacred geometry, which is what Stonehenge and the pyramids are also believed to have been based on. These layouts are used to enhance the power of the stones and can be used for a variety of reasons—not just for psychic skills. Some grids work by having crystals placed on the body, while others require having stones placed around a workspace. When used together in this manner, the stones resonate with one another and connect on a spiritual plane! You can change the vibration of a grid by adjusting the arrangement of the crystals.

This opens different energy fields and allows your own energy to be magnified.

Before forming any crystal grid, no matter the shape, be sure to thoroughly cleanse and empower your crystals (see pages 88–92). You should focus on your intention or question during the empowerment process.

Then, take a transparent crystal, such as clear quartz, and trace the outline of the grid around the crystals. This connects the energies of the stones to one another and activates them to work as a unit.

Crystals for Your Crown

To open your mind and boost your inner vision, you can use a simple grid called a crystal crown. For the sake of this introductory exercise, we'll choose amethyst, iolite, and clear quartz, which are malleable and work well both for protection and to enhance energetic combinations. We'll also need obsidian or black tourmaline.

Prepare a serene environment for yourself. Light some candles, burn incense, or use lavender (for relaxing) or peppermint (for energy) essential oils. Cleanse and empower your crystals (see pages 88–92), focusing on the question or issue around which you seek clarity. Breathe deeply while clearing all other thoughts.

Lie down on the bed and place the amethyst and iolite crystals next to each of your ears. Place the clear quartz on your forehead. In using this grid, you are balancing the hemispheres of your mind and allowing the crystal quartz to stabilize those energies.

You can also choose several other stones that will complement one another in this grid, such as desert rose agate (for intuition and mental calm) or Apache tears agate (for grounding, spiritual protection, and spiritual restoration) and place the entire group in a semicircle around your head.

To fully ground yourself, you should also place a black tourmaline or obsidian between your feet. This stone roots you to this world and keeps you safe during your mystical journey.

Direct your question to the universe and allow the answer to come to you in visions. You may see things that you don't understand at first, and that's all right. Allow every image to come and go without judgment or objection.

Give yourself a good ten to twenty minutes for this process. When the visions cease, write down what you observed in your mind's eye.

Again, some of the images may not make sense immediately, but in the coming days, they may take on new meaning!

Dream a Crystal Dream

For an easy psychic-enhancing grid, put your crystals underneath your pillow, or, if you think this will cause you to have a restless night, place them under your bed. Take care to cleanse and empower them first (see pages 88–92).

Prepare yourself for bed prior to putting your crystals in place for the night. Take a relaxing shower or bath, all the while contemplating that the stones' energy will work while you sleep, and envisioning that you will be open to the answers or visions that will come to you.

If you choose to place the crystals under your bed, don't just toss them underneath and hope for the best. Place them very deliberately, with thoughtfulness, directly under where you will be snoozing. Thank each stone as you place it for the work it will be doing for you.

Likewise, if the crystals are going under your pillow, give gratitude for each stone as you place it. Turn out the lights, relax, breathe deeply, and let the answers come to you in your sleep.

See chapter 11 for more on dream divination.

Crystal Sleep Mask

It's possible for your dreams to become disturbed after a psychic session. Sometimes you just can't shake energies loose right away, and they show up as vivid images in your sleep. If this happens, you can place a protective stone under your bed or pillow, or you can incorporate small pieces of a protective crystal into an eye mask to wear overnight.

Materials

A store-bought sleep mask with an elastic band

Fabric glue

A small piece of protective crystal

Ritual

Cleanse and empower your crystal (see pages 88–92), envisioning peaceful, undisturbed sleep as you do so. When ready, simply glue the crystal piece to your eye mask. It should be placed right around where your third eye chakra is—in the middle of your brow.

Wear this protective headgear when you go to sleep for as long as it takes your strange dreams to resolve.

Circles and Ovals

Circular or oval grids are very basic, simple grids to put together, but they are more dynamic than square or rectangular grids, as there is no beginning or end to the shape. Energy is free to flow and is not in danger of slowing or getting stuck in a corner. These grids can be large or small, depending on whether you plan to sit or lie down in the circle.

For the circular grid, you don't need to have scores of stones to make a complete circle—just enough to form the basic shape. Cleanse and empower your crystals (see pages 88–92), focusing on your intention as you do so. Place your crystals on the floor or on your bed in the desired shape. Once you've put your crystals down, step back to make sure you're happy with the grid and the order of the stones. This is your psychic force field, after all, and it needs to meet your standards!

An oval grid should consist of approximately six quartz crystals that are relatively large. Place the quartz in the following positions, which align with the chakras: one above your head, one below your feet, one at either side of the hips, one at either side of the arms.

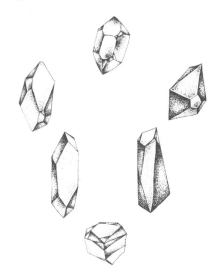

Lie in the oval's center and focus on the issue you're seeking clarity around. Have an open mind and heart in which to receive the answers.

Spirals and Stars

You can get creative with your grids and layouts—create a spiral or a star shape, or a rainbow or infinity shape. These shapes can be formed on a tabletop, as it may be difficult to place yourself in their centers.

Follow the same ritual as with any grid—cleanse and empower the stones prior to use (see pages 88–92), and then place your stones with intention, giving gratitude to each one.

In the case of a tabletop grid, you can write your intention and place it in the stone formation's center. You can place lit candles or other objects that hold special meaning to you into the layout as well. Tabletop grids can be left in place for as long as you like. Take care to visit the layout and focus on your intention daily.

Crystal Pyramids

You can also use a crystal pyramid to help develop your psychic abilities. A crystal pyramid is simply a crystal or stone that has been carved into the form of a pyramid. Smaller versions are quite affordable, depending on the variety of stone used, whereas larger pyramids can be higher in price. While crystal pyramids are not technically grids, the shape itself draws in and organizes spiritual energy so that you can access it in a focused form. You can use a large or small crystal pyramid for our purposes. Smaller stones can be held in your hands, while larger version can be used as a focal point.

If you are holding a small pyramid in your hands, close your eyes and focus on clearing your mind, which allows your psychic skills to expand. If you're using a large pyramid, soften your gaze while looking at the stone and allow the wisdom and knowledge you're seeking to come to you.

A Crystal Grid Spell for All-Seeing

Using a crystal grid is a great way to consolidate and boost an energetic field. You can use this energy for a lot of things—healing, mediation, cleansing, and, of course, psychic vision. Now that you know about arranging your crystals for maximum energy flow, let's talk about a special ritual that will work in conjunction with your precious stones to amplify and expand your psychic abilities.

Practitioners of magick know that spells are used only for positive intentions and that whatever you project to the universe, you will go on to receive once the affirmation returns to you. This spell for all-seeing is a magickal ritual that requires a bit of time and commitment.

Materials

Your crystal grid, using crystals of your choosing
(see list on pages 83–87 for inspiration)

Epsom salts

Several votive or tealight candles, in white

A crystal wand, using kyanite or clear quartz

A separate piece of crystal, of your choosing

Ritual

Cleanse and empower your crystals (see pages 88–92), and then form your crystal grid in the shape of your choice. Begin by setting your intention. Sit quietly and say to yourself, *"I am performing this ritual so that I can see what is unseen."* If there is a specific issue you want to know about, say something like:

"I want to see the person I will spend my life with."

Now prepare a cleansing bath with the Epsom salts, continuing to mediate on your intention all the while. This is a means of clearing your mind and cleansing any preconceived notions. Focus on purity of the mind during this time. Soak in the tub for at least twenty minutes, then rinse your body with clean water from the shower or spigot. Dry yourself with a clean towel.

Your spell-casting site can be set up indoors or outdoors, whichever is more comfortable and fills you with more inspiration. Light the candles, which will help to clear away any cluttered energy.

Hold the crystal wand in your dominant hand and the crystal of your choosing in the other hand. Point the wand at your grid and trace a line from one crystal to the next, activating the energy in the layout. Close your eyes and breathe deeply, again focusing on purity of vision and sharing in the crystals' energy.

Now recite the following spell (or create an incantation using your own words):

> *"Crystal power, strengthen my vision,*
> *So that I may know what is right and true.*
> *Loosen the ties that prevent me from knowing,*
> *Allow the messages to safely come through.*
> *Show me my future in front of my eyes,*
> *So that I may see, please be my guide.*
> *So mote it be."*

Thank the crystals for their assistance and let the crystal grid sit undisturbed. You can place the wand inside of the stone formation if you like. The spell is likely to manifest over the next few days, so during this time, try to pay attention to any visions that might come to you.

For even more powerful results, try practicing this spell outside under the light of a full moon.

WEARING CRYSTALS

An easy way to keep your psychic-boosting crystals nearby at all times is by wearing them. Not only will you sparkle and shine; you'll be able to easily draw upon whatever energy you need at that time. You can include magickal stones in any form of wearable accessory, such as bracelets, necklaces, earrings, rings, hair pieces, brooches, or belts.

Many diviners wear jewelry that contains a protective stone, as they are never sure what kind of forces they'll meet in a psychic session. Some of the best protective stones for this purpose are:

- **Black tourmaline**
- **Fluorite**
- **Hematite**
- **Kyanite**
- **Onyx**
- **Pyrite**

You can find crystal wearables of every style in New Age shops and any number of retailers, or you can craft your own.

Chapter 5

Tarot Magick

LEARNING TAROT CAN TAKE A WHILE BUT ONCE YOU
have mastered the art, it's a fantastic way to take a peek into the
future. Once you become proficient in the art of tarot readings,
you might even like to venture into it as a career. Tarot magick is a
relatively new practice but one fast becoming very popular due to its
pinpoint accuracy.

Using crystals alongside tarot only enhances the magick even more.
Crystals such as clear quartz will amplify the power of a reading, labradorite will enhance your psychic ability, and black obsidian will protect
you throughout the sitting. Always have a selection of stones nearby.

One very successful way to incorporate tarot into your magic is to use a chosen card to represent a situation you are spelling for. An example would be if you wanted to better your finances, you might place the Ace of Pentacles (the best money card in the deck) on to the altar while your spell is "cooking." Or, when performing spells for luck and happiness, you would select the two best cards in the deck (the Sun and the Ace of Cups) and rest them on the altar underneath your selected crystals.

The classic tarot deck has seventy-eight cards and contains four suits: Sands, Pentacles, Cups, and Swords. These four suits are known as the Minor Arcana and each include court cards, comprising Kings, Queens, Knights, and Pages. There are fifty-six suit cards in total. The remaining twenty-two cards are referred to as the Major Arcana.

DOING TAROT READINGS

Readings can be "cold," meaning that there is no specific issue being addressed, or they can be more focused, with the reader concentrating on a particular question in mind from the start. When you become proficient in the art of tarot readings, you can either read the cards for yourself or you can perform a translation for someone else.

One factor to keep in mind with the cards is that, although they each have particular significance, they can mean something entirely different when placed next to other cards in a spread. Some readers learn their skill from studying books, whereas others prefer to do more of a psychic reading, simply using the cards as a crutch.

Before bringing your cards out, prepare a crystal workspace. You can select crystals that you regularly work with or choose several from the list at the beginning of this chapter. Place the stones around the area where you will be performing your reading.

If you are carrying out a reading for yourself, then to begin, you must shuffle your deck for around three minutes. While you are doing this, focus on the questions you might have.

Because each card has multiple meanings (depending on whether it's drawn upright or reversed), it's perfectly acceptable for the cards to be mixed up every which way. After a good shuffle, split the deck into three equal piles with your left hand, then choose one of the three piles to work with before setting the other two piles to one side. Place the crystal(s) at the top of the workspace. Spread the cards out in a fan-like manner and, using any hand, make your selection. Try these simple layouts for tarot beginners:

Three-Card Spread: This is the most straightforward layout, but it can still give you useful information. This layout comprises only three cards, representing (from left to right): the past and influences affecting the current situation; the current situation; and the future.

Five-Card Spread: This is the three-card spread, but with two additional cards—one placed above, and one below, so that the layout resembles a cross. The card placed below signifies the causes of the current situation, and the card above represents the action to resolve it.

Horseshoe Spread: This is a seven-card spread in the shape of a semicircle. From left to right, the cards represent:

- The past
- The present
- Hidden influences
- The *querent*, or person having the reading
- Attitudes of the people surrounding the querent
- The action the querent should take
- The outcome

After the cards are in place, you can hold a crystal in one or both hands to help connect with your psychic vision. When you're done reading for someone else, you can cleanse yourself with a kyanite or selenite wand by simply waving it from top to bottom while envisioning a white light coming to clear any lingering energies.

When you are finished with your cards, you can cleanse and charge them along with your crystals. Just place a large crystal, like quartz, moonstone, amethyst, or kyanite, on top of the deck and then put it out in the moonlight overnight.

CHOOSING THE RIGHT DECK

I [Leanna] have found through the years that it's best when teaching students to start them on a traditional deck of tarot because it's better for them to learn the basics. Once they are more experienced, they can select different tarot packs for certain moods. There are quite a number of Wiccan decks to purchase and most witches will have six or seven different kinds.

Purchasing tarot decks can be tricky; in a shop, you can't take the cards out of their packaging to look at or hold them. It's best to research the images of the pack you might want to purchase online. Most decks come with a corresponding instructional booklet.

After buying your deck, smudge the cards with white sage and shuffle them for at least fifteen minutes. Spread them over a clean surface, placing crystals around them. Later wrap the deck in a silken scarf and when you go to bed, sleep with them under your pillow. You might want to buy a special box for them, which should be placed on a window ledge to keep them charged.

Do's and Don'ts—
The Keys to a Successful Reading

DON'TS

- Don't force anyone to have a reading
- Don't let anyone else use your tarot
- Don't let your children play with the deck
- Don't make dramatic predictions
- Don't eat or drink when conducting a reading
- Don't be too public while doing a reading (some people may think it's the work of the "devil")
- Don't read for strangers on your own
- Don't be spooked by your tarot predictions
- Don't be a party entertainer

DO'S

- Do place your cards outside in the moonlight to charge them
- Do keep them clean
- Do meditate before you begin to read
- Do be firm if you don't want to do a reading
- Do charge them with crystal power
- Do give hope in your readings
- Do experiment with different decks
- Do create your own spreads
- Do write down your predictions

INTERPRETING THE CARDS

Often when doing a reading you might notice something different about a card you hadn't noticed before, and this is good because it means your psychic energy is awakening. Take notice of it, as your interpretation may prove to be accurate in different ways. If, for instance, you look at the card of a Page and see a tear run down its face, then a child may be sad and unhappy and needs attention. You may be focusing on a Knight and sense there is a woman lurking in the background, which might indicate an illicit romance. Study the expressions of any animals in the cards: are they happy or going through an ordeal?

Some Difficult Cards to Read

There are certain cards that can be really difficult to place in a reading and can often baffle the reader. When learning tarot, it is best to always become familiar with these by learning as much as you can about them beforehand.

CARD NUMBER 0 OR 22:
The Fool
The card of innocence and naivety; but there is a need to look into things before leaping off the cliff. With positive cards in the spread, a new adventure is coming and

to trust in fate and destiny as life will
be changing in a big way. With negative
cards around, the Fool must take care
not to be led astray as wrong choices
could be his undoing.

CARD NUMBER 1:
The Magician
This card is one of pure magic and if
placed in any tarot spread will enhance
the reading. In modern tarot, a witch
considers him to be a powerful guide
who can help them on their journey of
discovery and soul wisdom.

CARD NUMBER 2:
The High Priestess
Many modern-day tarot readers
will use her as a muse or a guide,
especially for dream predictions. She
is, after all, the goddess of the moon,
the seer, the temple virgin. Her
titles are many. She brings magical
revelations and will always be a
blessing in a reading as she awakens
one's psychic abilities.

CARD NUMBER 6:
The Lovers, "Gemini"

Here we see a couple in love but choices have to be made. Do they stay together or perhaps go on to be separated? Look at the cards on either side of them. If the suit of cups and coins are in evidence, then all will be well. If rods or swords dominate, then a stormy relationship could ruin things. If this card is ever in the same spread as the Three of Swords or the Devil, then an infidelity is sure to take place.

CARD NUMBER 9:
The Hermit, "Virgo"

This gentle but powerful guide card also brings protection and represents the sign of Virgo. Because this is one of the cards that possesses an associated birth sign, you could also tell your client that the events predicted in the spread might take place around August and September. The Hermit is the benefactor of dream sleep; spellcast for him to be present in your dreams, especially if you are confused about your life. Take his card and place it next to your bed or even better, under your pillow.

CARD NUMBER 12:
The Hanged Man

This card looks sinister, as it depicts a man hanging upside down, strapped to a tree with one foot. In reality, it represents someone who is stuck and can't seem to move forward. If this card comes up during a reading for someone, it might mean things might take a whole year before moving on to better times; tell the querent not to give up hope and just be patient.

CARD NUMBER 13:
Death, "Scorpio"

The Grim Reaper is skeletal, the stuff of nightmares, and with certain swords present in the spread, such as the Nine or Ten of Swords, it can predict a death. In a spread with no swords however, this predicts a time of new beginnings: off with the old and on with the new. You can also use this card as a dating time of Scorpio, meaning the predictions could arise around the winter months or around October, November.

CARD NUMBER 15:
The Devil, "Capricorn"

This card represents the sign of Capricorn, depicting a half-man, half-goat god. This card can symbolize decadence or debauchery—this could indicate a temptation toward worldly pleasures or vices such as drugs, alcohol, sex, or even violence. It could also signal that a person is being held fast and unwilling to change. In a spread with positive cards around it, then there is hope ahead to break free.

CARD NUMBER 16:
The Tower

The Tower is the most complex card in the deck and it's hard to find anything positive to link it with. It has many meanings: suicidal tendencies, split personality, rages, drugs, and depravity. But if a positive card, such as the Sun or the Ace of Cups is beside it, then brilliant solutions will be found. If next to the Lovers, then a violent controlling relationship could be ruining someone's life. It would be wise to use spellcraft for added protection and strength.

CARD NUMBER 18:

The Moon, "Pisces"

A mysterious card; indicates that things may be hidden from the querent, especially when objects or money go missing. Trust no one; tell the querent to go outside when the moon is full and ask it to clarify things for them. All is not what it seems.

CARD NUMBER 20:

Judgement

This is the card of karma: what goes around comes around. The Judgement card asks the seeker to become wise and deepen their soul's knowledge. If a person has no respect for others or possesses bad habits like smoking or drinking, they must be worked upon, especially if the querent believes in reincarnation. Most witches agree that such habits, if still present at death, could mean having to return to the earth plane to try again. Better to get it right the first time.

The Nightmare Fives

As a tarot reader of thirty years, I [Leanna] have always found the Fives in the Minor Arcana to be meddlesome. They are niggling little cards that can bring sadness and disruption. If they all appear in one reading, the querent could be in for a tough time ahead.

FIVE OF SWORDS: Health issues and blood tests, not to mention arguments and spite.

FIVE OF CUPS: Family and marital conflict, sibling rivalry.

FIVE OF WANDS: In the workplace there could be upsets and rows with demanding bosses or colleagues.

FIVE OF PENTACLES: A lack of cash and wondering if those bills will get paid. Fretting over the elderly or the sick.

As there are a lot of friction connected with these cards, it might be an idea to open all the doors and windows to get some fresh air into the house; if its blowy, all the better. Once this has been done, light a white sage stick and smudge the property, even the toilets and cupboards, to dispel any negativity. Keep repeating, *"I cleanse and bless this space."*

Using Two Different Decks in a Spread

Once a person is proficient in tarot they might want to experiment in this way. Use a traditional pack, such as the Morgan Greer. Shuffle and place the cards into a large circle, called the American Sundial. Then shuffle the second deck and create another circle inside of the first one. In the center space, place crystals and favorite herbs to enhance the reading.

When all the cards are in situ, ring Tibetan bells or a little hand bell over the cards and smudge the area lightly with white sage incense. Start the reading from the top of the large circle and continue clockwise (this is usually for a yearly prediction). The inner circle can be used for the enlightenment of the soul, improving one's magical abilities, and learning lessons in life. It is a good idea to write down the whole reading in your Book of Shadows for future reference or record it on your phone.

Chapter 6

Pendulum Divining

AH, QUESTIONS, QUESTIONS, QUESTIONS. ALL OF US are plagued by the unknown from time to time. Should I take this new job or hold out for a better offer? Should I sign a lease for this apartment or keep looking? Is this new love interest worth my while, or am I kidding myself? Is Monday the best day to fly standby, or should I wait until Tuesday . . . or maybe Thursday? At times, we all have a nagging sense that something we were planning or thinking about doing does not feel quite right.

Maybe you aren't sure why you don't want to travel on a certain day, for example, but you just know the idea isn't sitting well with you. It could be that you're remembering the strange guy you had to sit next to on your last flight, or it could be just your imagination going wild. But often our intuition reports back to us with a little tug on the sleeve, as if to say, "Hey! Pay attention! I need to tell you something!"

For those of us who are in tune with our intuitive side, the simple little tool that is the pendulum can help us dig deeper into our inner self and be guided by our inner voice in finding the best paths to follow. Using the pendulum is actually a form of *dowsing*, which is also sometimes called divining. If you're familiar with these terms, you might envision someone running around Death Valley with a forked stick, looking for water. That is one form of dowsing, the one that for some reason sticks in the public's mind. In fact, dowsing with a pendulum is a much more common practice than using a stick or divining rod, and there are many other methods as well. While you can certainly use a pendulum to seek water, it is more commonly used to divine truth, to balance energy, to cleanse the chakras, or to make contact with the spiritual plane for any number of reasons.

Dowsing itself is simply a means of using your body's own intuition and reflexes to understand what's happening in your life and in your environment. In interpreting your readings, you're really just learning to look at things in a new way—a way that's always been accessible to you, though perhaps you weren't actively using it before.

THE PENDULUM,
PAST AND PRESENT

Dowsing has been around forever. There are indications that it was used many centuries ago to appease the gods, to predict the future, to find auspicious times for sowing and reaping, and to be judge and jury in matters of the law (specifically, in determining a suspect's guilt or innocence).

In 1326, Pope John XXII authorized the prosecution of sorcerers as devil-worshipping heretics and forbade divining as an act of sorcery. There are no statistics on how many Catholics continued to perform dowsing rituals in secret, but since the practice has survived to this day, it was likely more than a few. (It is also not clear why the Pope thought Satan would waste his time answering questions about such matters as the best time to plant a harvest.)

An old wives' tale says that the pendulum can predict the sex of an unborn baby. A dowser or psychic would tie the pregnant woman's wedding ring to a length of string and dangle it over her big belly. The ring's movement was supposed to indicate a boy or a girl (if a pendulum swung to the left, it was a boy; to the right, a girl). In Britain the same method is still used today, but the ring is replaced with a threaded needle. See more about how to interpret the swing of the pendulum later in this chapter.

IN PURSUIT OF THE PERFECT PENDULUM

A pendulum is an object that hangs on a string or chain. The object can be made of wood, metal, plastic, or even a string. It can be adorned with crystals or unadorned. The weight of the object is not important. Most dowsers will tell you that it's important to find a pendulum you will be comfortable with.

Some pendulums come on a very long chain. This can make people with shorter arms feel as though they really can't interpret what the weight is doing, because it's simply hanging too low. Gather up as much of the chain as needed in order to read the movements of the pendulum.

Pendulums are not hard to come by. Most metaphysical stores stock them, and you can also purchase them easily online. They are available in every price range, from under $10 to over $100. Think of it as choosing a wise new friend, one you'll be seeking guidance and advice from. This is not a decision to make quickly or lightly. It's just like selecting a crystal for yourself; you have to feel a genuine connection to get the best results.

Pendulum Properties

So you waltz into your local metaphysical shop, ready to adopt the perfect pendulum, and you look into the jewelry case only to find there are over fifty to choose from. All colors, all sizes—how do you begin the process of elimination?

First, ask the shopkeeper for help. Most men and women who work in these stores are extremely knowledgeable about the products and how to use them, and most are also eager to share their own experiences. Listen to what they have to say, but keep in mind that the pendulum is a very personal experience, so what works well for one person may not work for you.

Pendulums come in all weights, shapes, and designs. Generally speaking, beginners should start with a medium weight. The theory is that a pendulum that's too light can pick up too many energies and send mixed messages. A too-heavy weight can be difficult to learn with because it takes longer for the pendulum to gain momentum, which means that its reaction time is slower. This could leave you feeling frustrated.

The shape you choose will depend on what you want to use it for:

- **SPIRAL:** A pointy-ended, spiral-shaped weight, used for answering general life questions.

- **TRIANGULAR:** This kind of pendulum picks up the vibration of numbers, and is great for use in numerology or choosing lottery numbers.

- **SEPHOROTON:** A pendulum that has a circular center and a pointed bottom. This unique shape is supposed to cut down on errant vibrations and give clear answers to questions about health, love, and money.

- **MERKABA:** A star-shaped pendulum that incorporates sacred geometry in its design to unite the body, soul, and spirit. This union creates an energetic field called the Merkaba effect.

- **CHAKRA:** A stone pendulum whose chain contains seven stones representing the seven chakras (the body's energy centers). Used to find and repair an imbalance in one or more of the chakras.

- **OSIRIS:** A long pendulum with four "hemispheres" stacked on top of each other. This design is meant to amplify the pendulum's sensitivity, and the osiris is considered to be a very powerful tool. It is used to research electromagnetic fields and gain insight into astrological charts.

- **CHAMBERED:** A hollow pendulum that you can place energetic crystals inside for greater power and clarity. If you're asking the pendulum a question about another person, you can also place a strand of that person's hair in the chamber.

Now let's talk about the materials that many pendulums are made of, the energy qualities of different stones and crystals, and why you might choose one over another (for more information about crystals and stones, see chapter 4, "Crystal Divination"):

AMETHYST Used in meditation, channeling, and focusing psychic abilities. It gives a feeling of peace and connects you with your spiritual side.

BLOODSTONE The stone of courage, promoting centering, grounding, and balance. This is a good stone to use for anxiety or emotional stress.

CITRINE Clears negative energy in a big way! After using citrine, you may notice you feel more optimistic, energetic, focused, and confident. Citrine also attracts abundance (which can go a long way toward making you feel more optimistic and confident).

FLUORITE Promotes stability, order, balance, and healing, and it is a great stone for use in matters where clarity and objectivity are important. Fluorite doesn't absorb energy the way other stones do, so it gives pretty reliable responses.

HEMATITE Contains grounding properties; offers protection from negative energies.

HONEY CALCITE Stimulates positive energy for personal goals.

LAPIS LAZULI Connects the physical and celestial planes, increasing wisdom and otherworldly knowledge, awareness, and intuition. Lapis lazuli is also a stone of protection.

MOONSTONE Emits a feminine energy, supporting balance, intuition, and good judgment. Moonstone is also used to balance the female reproductive system and to protect travelers on their journeys.

QUARTZ A universal stone, which means that it responds well to whatever purpose you assign it. It draws, activates, stores, transmits, and multiplies all kinds of energetic forces, so no matter what you're using a quartz pendulum for—questions of love, money, social responsibility, research—you can't go wrong.

ROSE QUARTZ Sometimes recommended for women, as it has a special vibration that reacts well to feminine energy. Rose quartz emits love, compassion, and forgiveness, promotes creativity and confidence, and heals emotional and sexual issues.

RUBY Enhances positive energy for personal goals.

SELENITE Helps with psychic energy and mental clarity.

SMOKY QUARTZ Wards off negative energy; promotes grounding and prosperity.

Remember that an inexpensive pendulum will work just as well as a pricier version. The crux of the matter really is in learning to focus and concentrate your energy. Although there are purists out there who believe that you should only use certain crystals or shapes for certain purposes, most people say that choosing and using a pendulum is a very personal thing. In other words, if you find that a pendulum is responding well for you, don't worry so much about its material, shape, or price. As with all things spiritual, it's best to just go with the flow.

GET TO KNOW YOUR PENDULUM

The pendulum responds to your energetic field, but because it's a piece of rock, crystal, metal, or wood hanging from a chain, it also responds to gravity and reflexes. Obviously, you don't want to set the stone swinging by a flick of the wrist or a flinch of the fingers, so learning to hold the pendulum is an important step.

This is key; we don't want you to get false readings and then decide that the pendulum is a bogus tool. Don't buy into skeptics' beliefs that there is nothing beyond this earthly realm, that believers in the mystical planes create their own answers. The etheric realm is real, and you can tap into it.

To hold the pendulum correctly, position the chain between your thumb and forefinger, allowing the weight to dangle. If your pendulum has a long chain, it's perfectly all right to shorten it by holding it closer to the pendulum. Shortening the length also shortens response time.

Even though you should be friendly and comfortable with your pendulum, a pendulum session calls for a certain amount of focus and respect as well. Begin every session by settling into a quiet, calm space. Clear your mind. Invite your spirit guides and angels to join and assist you. Envision yourself surrounded by a white light, and say a simple, silent prayer for protection.

Start by sitting at a table and stabilizing your elbow on the surface. Begin to physically move your pendulum forward and backward.

Remember that the pendulum does not respond to your mental urgings; instead, it responds to your energy. Negative, skeptical energy will result in negative findings. Positive, relaxed energy is what you want to put out for the best results.

When you're relaxed and your mind is clear and focused, ask your pendulum questions that it can answer "yes" to, easy things such as "Is it raining today?" or "Is my shirt pink?" Take note of how the pendulum responds to these easy queries. That's your "yes" motion. Once it starts moving, ask the pendulum to show you an even stronger "yes," perhaps by asking it, "Is my name _____?" so that there's no mistaking its movement. But if you don't get a more pronounced motion, don't fret.

Now, ask the pendulum some "no" questions, like "Is my hair red?" (if you happen to be blond) or "Is today Saturday?"

when you know it is Monday. Then ask it a "maybe" question, such as "Will I talk to my friend Joe today?" Notice how your pendulum reacts to these questions too.

The movement of the pendulum is obviously limited by physical factors, but you may discern several types of motion. Here's what to look for when you're waiting for an answer:

- A side-to-side swinging
- A diagonal swinging
- A clockwise or counterclockwise rotation
- A "jump"

Will your "yes" movement be the same from now until the end of time? Does the pendulum ever change its mind? Movements do change from time to time, so every now and then, especially once you really know your pendulum, retest it with your easy questions, just to make sure you're getting the same results. If you are a collector of pendulums, don't expect every one of them to be the same. You will need to establish these yes and no movements with each pendulum you own.

If you want more of a visual response, you can hold the pendulum over a mat or card with answers printed on it. You can buy these or make these—though if you do create one on your own, make sure you leave plenty of room between the answer areas so you aren't confused by the pendulum's movements. One simple version of this mat has YES printed on the top and bottom, NO on the sides, and MAYBE in two diagonal corners. This setup encourages the pendulum to move in certain directions according to its responses.

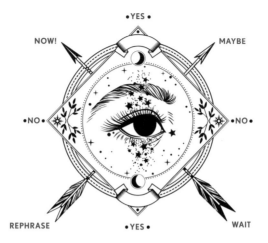

YES

NOW!   MAYBE

NO   NO

REPHRASE   YES   WAIT

Ask Anything (but Ask the Right Way)

You can ask your pendulum almost anything, but the way you phrase the question is important when it comes to understanding the larger picture. You have to understand that the pendulum can only give you "yes" and "no" answers, so it's pointless asking it something lengthy or intricate. This will just confuse matters, and you may not get any results at all.

For example, if you ask, "Should I buy a house now?" and the answer is "no," don't give up. You might be able to find out more by rephrasing your question. Try "Should I buy a house in the winter?" and see what happens. If you need to, go through each season and see which one the pendulum responds positively to.

Sometimes the pendulum won't swing at all, but just hang there, showing no movement. This usually occurs when it doesn't know the answer to your question or when, for whatever reason, you are not supposed to know the outcome of a situation. You just have to accept this and change your subject to ask it something else.

If you make your questions as clear and concise as possible, the pendulum can more or less get to the bottom of anything:

- Questions about significant others
- Where to go on vacation
- Which outfit to wear to a job interview
- How much money to invest
- The best time to have children
- What kind of pet you should adopt
- Which career path to follow
- If you will get married this year

You can even ask the best day to play golf or the best movie to see. There is *no question that's off limits!*

Important Points to Remember

- **Ask one question at a time.** Don't ask, "Should I adopt a dog or cat?" In a situation like this, break that into two questions.

- **Do not make it overly complicated.** Simplify the question "Should I bring a coat tonight because it might rain?" into either "Should I take a coat with me tonight?" or "Is it going to rain tonight?"

- **Try to phrase questions in a positive light.** Change "Did I make the wrong choice in the car I bought?" to "Did I make the right decision in buying my new car?"

- **After you've determined the meanings of your pendulums movements,** don't continue asking questions to which you already know the answers. This is game-playing and can lead to confusing results due to your own mixed-up energy!

Angel Protection

When you work with the pendulum, it doesn't usually tap into the lower vibrations, so there is little danger of invoking any unwanted spirits. However, when you are working with any form of divination, it is nice to begin your spiritual session with a silent prayer for protection. You can do this by simply closing your eyes and asking your angel to protect you from anything negative and to surround you with a positive light.

GOING FURTHER

To gain insight into more involved questions, you can create a chart populated with possible appropriate responses. Pie charts tend to work best, as they give the pendulum a central starting point and easy access to every potential answer. Should you have three job offers on the table and want to know which is the best fit, you would draw a pie chart with each option represented as an equal slice. Leave a small circle in the center of the chart as a neutral starting point.

Decide what kind of information you want.

- **Which job should you take?**
- **Which company will present the most opportunity for your career?**
- **Which company will have the most relaxed atmosphere?**
- **Which job will feel most rewarding?**

Using a chart gives you the latitude to get more creative with your questions. The chart can contain as many pieces of information as you need. Want to know what kind of flowers you should plant? You can slice your circular chart into twenty pieces if you so desire. Just make sure that you are allowing enough space for each option so you can clearly interpret your answers.

SWING INTO BETTER HEALTH

The pendulum is also used to single out health and emotional issues, many of which are believed to be tied to the chakras, or the energy centers of the body. Pendulum energy can pinpoint imbalances in the chakras so that they can be restored to good health.

Chakra is a Sanskrit word meaning "wheel" or "turning." Both yogic Hindu and Tantric Buddhist philosophies teach that every human has these wheels of energy at seven specific points in the body along a column that goes from the base of the spine to the top of the head.

FIRST CHAKRA:
Base or Root Chakra

Located at the base of the spine; relates to feelings of survival and feeling grounded. Imbalance makes you feel as though you have to fight to survive or as though you have no real grounding place.

SECOND CHAKRA:
Sacral Chakra

Located near the ovaries in women, near the prostate in men; associated with sexual health. Blockage results in emotional issues or sexual guilt.

THIRD CHAKRA:
Solar Plexus Chakra

Around the navel and lower torso; relates to feeling powerful in your surroundings. An imbalance makes you feel victimized, angry, and powerless.

FOURTH CHAKRA:
Heart Chakra

Right where you'd expect it to be. Relates to feeling loved and at peace. An imbalance can actually manifest as heart or immune problems or lead you to feel as though you lack compassion for others.

FIFTH CHAKRA:
Throat Chakra

Throat and neck region; linked to feelings of
creativity and communication. Imbalance happens
when you can't make yourself heard, and it
manifests as discomfort in this area.

SIXTH CHAKRA:
Brow or Third Eye Chakra

In the center of the forehead (pineal gland or third
eye); relates to psychic abilities, imagination, and
dreaming. An imbalance could result in writer's
block or a general lack of ideas or vision.

SEVENTH CHAKRA:
Crown Chakra

Located on the top of the head, associated with
spiritual connection, understanding, and bliss.
Imbalance results in feelings of floundering or just
not knowing what you believe.

The chakras are the points for the gathering and transmitting of
energy in the body, and as long as they are clear and balanced, *you'll* feel
clear and balanced. If a chakra becomes imbalanced or blocked with
negative energy, then you're going to feel it, either physically (as with a

blocked throat chakra) or emotionally (as with a blocked crown chakra). But all is not lost! The pendulum can help to clear those problem areas, leaving you as balanced as an Olympic gymnast.

So how do you determine which chakras are clear as a bell and which are stagnant? You'll need a partner for this exercise—one who is not self-conscious and who doesn't mind sprawling out in a prone position. First you will assess your friend's chakras. Have your friend lie down face up on the floor or a bed, and sit beside them. Both of you should close your eyes and breathe to focus your energy and clear your minds of distractions. When you're both ready, begin by holding your pendulum over your friend's root chakra. (It's actually located near their rear end, but you can access the energy by holding it over their genital region . . . which is why you shouldn't choose a shy friend for this experiment.) Ask, "Is this chakra in balance?" Repeat the question until the answer becomes clear. Take note of the response, then move up the body, asking the same question over the other six chakras. Use the chakra list on pages 134–35 to interpret what's going on with your friend.

If you should find that a chakra is out of whack, take your pendulum and move it in a clockwise motion over the area. This "stirs" the chakra, allowing whatever is stuck to begin moving and, hopefully, to be cleared out.

Now ask your friend to perform the same sequence of steps to evaluate your chakras.

THE CARE AND FEEDING
OF YOUR PENDULUM

It is important to keep your pendulum clean, especially if it is made of crystal. A monthly cleansing is usually all it needs, but if you are using it to balance chakras, then we advise you to go through the cleansing procedure outlined below after each session.

Now, I have to make this clear: You can't cleanse your pendulum by tossing it into the dishwasher or leaving it in the pocket of your dirty jeans when you're doing the laundry. Of course, use a soft cloth to wipe off any smudges or dust, but be aware that energetic forces are the toughest "stains" you'll ever have to remove from your pendulum, so it must be done right. You'll need to use the strongest elements at your disposal—the elements of nature:

- **EARTH:** Simply bury your pendulum in soil, sand, or sea salt and just let it sit for a few hours. (You can even do this indoors using a bowl. Also see page 89 for a note about certain stones that should not be used with salt.) The negative energies will be released and absorbed into the earthen element. If you do bury the pendulum in a bowl, just make sure to get rid of the soil, sand, or salt when you're finished. Take it outside and pour it right onto the earth.

- **FIRE:** Place your pendulum in direct sunlight early in the morning. Let it sit until sundown to allow the positive energy to take hold.

- **WATER:** This method requires a glass of water that's been energized by a crystal. (To do this, we recommend placing a crystal of quartz in a container of water and letting it soak for about twelve hours.) Put your pendulum in the energized water and allow it to sit in there for several hours.

- **AIR:** Light a sandalwood incense stick and pass the pendulum through its smoke three times. Since you are directly involved in this process, you need to really focus on the task at hand, saying a prayer for cleansing or blessing or just stating your intent. When the pendulum feels light and solid (as opposed to heavy or "fuzzy"), the cleansing is complete.

YOUR FUTURE IS IN MOTION

When using your pendulum to make decisions, you're going to feel a sense of control over your world that's nothing less than amazing. Why should a stone or crystal make you feel as though you're finally seeing things for what they are and what they can be? Because the pendulum is just a means of putting you in touch with what you already know. So connect with that knowledge, let it out, use it! And when people start saying things like "Mary is so wise, so in touch with her feelings, so confident about where she's headed in life," you can either share your little secret . . . or just share a little smile.

Chapter 7

Palmistry

THE ART OF PALMISTRY (ALSO CALLED CHIROMANCY or chirosophy), is believed to have at least some origin in Hinduism. Many cultures adopted palmistry, so there are different meanings in every background. Irish astrologer William John Warner, popularly known as Cheiro, studied with masters in India and brought a renewed popularity to the practice in Western Europe in the early twentieth century. Much of what we think of as modern palmistry is based on Cheiro's work. Palmistry is a vast, technical subject that warrants a book all its own. It is so involved that to read a palm properly from a print or a photocopy would take many hours.

Every line on your palm is like a map of your life, and because everyone's life is different, no two palms are the same. The following information is merely a bite-size chunk of some of the basics in the Western and Vedic traditions. Many witches will select Vedic palmistry as a tool for divination.

Note: To do a palmistry reading correctly, prints of the hands are a must—or a good photocopy of the palms will do just as well. If the photocopy is in color, all the better for skin textures and health areas. It will allow you to dwell on every little nuance of the palm. This is when focus is placed on hand markings and initials.

HANDS

First you can start by assessing the size of the hand in proportion to the body type.

BIG HANDS Sensitive, creative, and naturally inquisitive. People with large hands have an eye for detail that small-handed people may miss. For example, they can be adept at jewelry making, mending watches, and tool-making.

In Love: A good mix for marriage but inclined to be quiet and watchful of others, a person of few words, but one who is loyal and loves deeply.

MID-SIZE HANDS People with mid-size hands usually go with the flow. They don't get angry, they don't hang on to grudges, and they aren't prone to mood swings. They want peace in life and seek it out diligently.

In Love: These owners are laid back and will strive for harmony in their relationship. They will hate to row or bicker with their spouse. When family matters are difficult, they will be a strong support.

SMALL HANDS These people are sometimes a pain to live with because they are inclined to be over and their tempers can suddenly flare. Having an impatient personality, they will detest muddle and mess. Being house proud, their common expression will be "wipe your feet!"

On the plus side, these folks are focused and determined.

In Love: Sometimes demanding and can nag for perfection from their partner.

Now, take a look at the shape of the hand.

THICK, SQUARE HANDS These types are often work-oriented, but not great philosophers. They prefer not to get embroiled in too many deep thoughts because they'd rather be doing something energetic. They are no-nonsense and level-headed and will support their families by putting food on the table and being a good parent. Square hands belong to practical people who often work outdoors.

THIN NARROW HANDS This hand type can belong to narrow-minded folks who take time to adjust to a new way of thinking. They will lavish themselves with gifts but can be mean when buying for others. They are inclined to overthink things and harbor memories from the past, so they forget nothing. These folks can be quite moody, and (sometimes) unkind, but they are also logical and find practical solutions to problems.

FINGERS

Next take a look at the fingers:

MEDIUM FINGERS These represent balance in most areas and usually belong to well-rounded individuals.

LONG FINGERS Instead of ruminating on situations and ideas, long-fingered folks tend to act without a lot of thought and sometimes find themselves in a real mess because of it. These people tend to operate on emotion and may miss important facts.

SHORT FINGERS Nimble people generally have short fingers. They are those who think and act quickly, and usually with good judgment.

Names of Fingers

Each one of the fingers, not including the thumb, is named as follows:

FOREFINGER OR INDEX—JUPITER Jupiter represents career and idealism. If this finger is long, it can mean the person may be likely to venture into self-employment; this could be anything from a small business to a chain of companies. If the Jupiter finger is shorter, it shows a lack of ambition and someone who suffers from no self-confidence.

MIDDLE FINGER—SATURN Saturn symbolizes psychology. If this finger is long, the owner likes privacy and solitude and has a love of learning. If short, this person could be regarded as thoughtless or careless.

RING FINGER—APOLLO When the Apollo finger is long, its owner will have a love of beauty or lean toward fame and fortune. They will also be cultured, having a fondness for history and the arts. These are loving individuals who delight in helping children progress. If it is overly long, the owner may have a little bit of an ego and be a risk-taker. Although academically clever, they will enjoy money or may even take up gambling.

LITTLE FINGER—MERCURY A long Mercury finger shows a good communicator, whereas a short or stocky finger signals the reverse, making it difficult for the owner to correspond with others socially. If the finger is crooked, the person is secretive. If particularly pointy, you are looking at a psychic type.

Fingernails

The average nail takes twelve weeks to grow from cuticle to tip, so fingernails tell us a lot about the state of health for an individual at the time. The size and shape of the nails can reveal a lot about a person as well. Healthy nails tend to be smooth and supple, with pink skin underneath and a small whitish moon or semicircle at its base. Pockmarks, striations, and cracks are not healthy and indicate something is amiss with that person's health. Additionally, if you see redness in the nail, the owner might suffer from psychological or emotional disorders, often stemming from an addictive nature.

Here's how to read basic nail shapes:

SMALL NAILS These are energetic people generally, but they can have a hot-tempered or impulsive nature. They are pernickety, exacting, and always striving toward perfection. Everything in their home will have a place and a purpose. They possess a witty personality and are often somewhat opinionated. Nails such as these might also tell us that the person is a nervous type or high-strung.

LARGE or SQUARE NAILS This nail type belongs to hard-working achievers with a sense of confidence. These people are generally in excellent health, likely to have stamina and determination. They do tend to be stubborn at times and can get fidgety and restless, never sitting still. The owner of these nails can often be prone to minor accidents and could suffer from back problems pertaining to the shoulders and neck areas.

OVAL or ALMOND NAILS The nicest of all nail shapes, these individuals are kind, friendly, open-hearted, and mild-mannered. They are also open to new people and ideas and will do anything to relieve the stress of others. They shy away from confrontation, preferring to keep the peace at all times. People with these nail shapes are often prone to diabetes or allergies.

WIDE or FAN-SHAPED These people can hold a nervous disposition and will use up their energy very quickly. They have a daydreamy character and crave stability in life, are loyal to the hilt and thrive on routine. However, they dislike any kind of change and have a strong aversion to criticism.

READING THE PALM LINES

The palm has four main lines: **the heart line, head line, life line, and fate line.**

Heart Line

This is the prominent line located directly underneath the fingers, running to the edge of the palm under the Mercury finger. The heart line relates to anything representing affairs of the heart, be it emotional health or romantic inclinations. A deep heart line belongs to someone who is creative, artistic, and caring. If the heart line connects with attachment lines, this person will always be the boss in a relationship and have the upper hand. If you see a short heart line, the owner will be very down to earth and single-minded in their approach to relationships. A weak or broken heart line can mean this person has had their heart broken at some point, but this also tells of inconsistency in love or the possibility of unfaithfulness. This person might fall in love with people who are already married or in relationships and often becomes a victim.

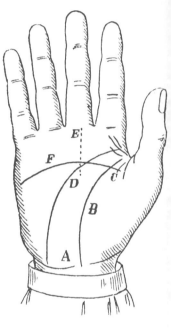

A *chained* line, or a line often intersected by other lines, indicates someone who feels emotions deeply and expresses themselves effectively—maybe a little too effectively at times. The chained line also suggests that this person loves to be in love and is perhaps too free with their heart. Circles on this line mean that the owner will have to take care of their health, as there could be serious health problems later. Purple dots and dashes can be linked to heart problems, especially if the querent is overweight.

Nowadays it is common to see a short twig or fork at the beginning of the heart line, sitting directly below the Saturn, or middle, finger. This indicates divorce or separation from a long-term relationship. If the twig has multiple branches, it would indicate more than one separation.

Head Line

The head line is located underneath the heart line, running across the palm toward the outer edge of the hand, or Percussion. This line depicts the person's interest in knowledge and learning. A long head line indicates that the person is not only curious but also perceptive, intelligent, and witty. A short or abbreviated line means that this person has a short attention span and probably has trouble completing projects. A long sloping headline is indicative if the head line is merged to the life line, there is a firm attachment to family; this person might stay in the family home, lacking the courage to become independent and leave the nest. When the head line is separate from the life line and a gap forms between the two, the person will be fiercely independent and will probably leave home early in life.

Chains on the head line are not a good sign, indicating that this person can be inclined toward cluster headaches or general problems with the head, especially neck and shoulder strain. These people may tire quickly, suffer insomnia, or lack energy generally. A break in the head line tells us that the individual will have to take care of accidents, especially if there is a cross on the line. To spot a divorce on the hand, the head line will form a twig or fork underneath the first finger. In Vedic palmistry, if the head line is long and sloping, the person will be on a spiritual quest and will have a fascination for witchcraft and practice meditation and healing. The palmist would surmise them to be an old soul reincarnating to help others.

Life Line

The life line surrounds the base of the thumb, the Mount of Venus, in a semicircle. It indicates a person's energy level, their physical health, and how they're doing in the larger scheme of life.

Many people look at the length of the life line to predict how long someone will live. Although that is true to a point, the lines in our hands can grow as we get older, so someone could start out with a short, weak line and go on to possess a much stronger, lengthier line in years to come. The deeper the line, the higher the energy level and the happier the life. If the line is weedy or frail, the owner might suffer from unhappiness and be apathetic.

Look at both hands. It is said that the left hand is what the gods give you and the right hand is what you do with your life. If you are left-handed, this saying is reversed. Therefore, if you are a heavy smoker or drinker, or dabble in drugs, the life line on your opposite hand would be shorter. One of Leanna's family members who was right-handed had a long lifeline on her left hand but on her right hand it was considerably shorter. Sadly, she was an alcoholic and had smoked since her teenage years. So, in effect she took away her long lifeline.

If someone has a life line that is interrupted or ends abruptly, that does not mean they are doomed to a short life; it might indicate a tendency toward worry and anxiety. A break in the line can often communicate life changes, such as a brand-new journey or a massive change in circumstance. A deep, red line illustrates a sexy, passionate individual who enjoys a healthy libido.

Fate Line

This line usually runs directly down the center of the hand from the Saturn, or middle, finger to the base of the wrist, which we call the *rascette* line; the fate line can then go off in different directions, bending to either the left or the right. It is a true indicator of character and gives us a great deal of information regarding the owner's destiny. A long, unbroken fate line indicates a person who strives forward in life and has a good work ethic. In Vedic palmistry, the length of the person's life can be measured in conjunction with the life line.

If the line travels toward the Jupiter, or index, finger, it shows signs of career success—but often at the expense of a relationship. If it leans more toward Saturn, the middle finger, then the owner will be more successful in life after a time of hard work and effort. Lines that cross the fate line horizontally foretell a difficult life, often troubled with bad luck. Some interpretations see this as more of a spiritual sign, showing that the person is striving for wisdom in life by learning hard lessons.

Mystic Cross

The space between the heart line and head line is called the *quadrangle* and resembles a small runway. If a small cross appears between these two lines, you are looking at someone with a natural psychic ability. This is called a *mystic cross*. A perfect cross will sit directly in the center of the quadrangle without any of its four points touching either the heart or head lines. Imperfect crosses do not mean that the owner is not psychic; rather, they simply imply that the level of psychic ability is not as strong. If you run your finger from the top of the Saturn, or middle, finger down to the base of your wrist, your finger should pass through this cross. It is quite rare to have one of these, but lots of witches do tend to own one, probably because they take such an interest in the esoteric practices!

Because the art of palm reading has worldly roots, there are different interpretations of the structures of the palm. It's best to learn what you can at a slow pace, practice, and then trust your own instincts.

Children's Lines

Through the years, children's lines have caused a lot of interest in palmistry and also controversy. Children's lines sit underneath the little finger on the Mercury Mount. These can appear as tiny upright or slanted lines which can be deep set or faint. Straight upright lines are supposed to represent male children, and slanting lines, girls. As far as accuracy is concerned, it is debatable. Some days the theory works on clients, other days not so good. The more lines there are, the more children the querent *should* have.

Deanna's Unicorns

Palm reading is about discovering an individual's personality and often advising them as to what they can achieve. I once met a woman who came for a reading and told her she was creative and should learn to do sculpture, as her Apollo finger indicated this. She looked at me quizzically and exclaimed, "What? I haven't got a creative bone in my body!" Later she joined a sculpting course, and the teacher said "What do you want to sculpt?" Her reply was, "I don't really know, but a palmist told me to come." After a while they decided a horse's head would be a good start and as soon as she had the clay in her hands, she was inspired to create the most wonderful unicorn. In my conservatory, I have two of her unicorn busts, which I feel so privileged to own. Later the woman went on to take commissions and held exhibitions of her work.

Relationship Lines

These are housed on the percussion or striking part of the hand, underneath the Mercury finger, and the lines sit in the Mercury Mount near the children's lines.

Travel Lines

These are also found on the full percussion side of the hand, and each dash represents a different country. The more lines you have, the more countries you will travel to.

Hand Health

Please remember if you see these conditions, you *are not a doctor* so take care with how you present your opinion. When a palmist examines a person's hand much can be gleaned by the color, texture, and appearance.

RED PALMS A bright red mottled palm is an indication that the person could be a heavy drinker or perhaps suffer from an allergy. Ask them to drink more water and watch their liver. In females, this can also represent someone who has a hormone imbalance so they might suffer with painful menstrual cycles or have heavy periods.

PALE HANDS PALMS that have little color can be a warning that the person is anemic. They may need to watch their diet more carefully or begin a healthy eating plan.

ORANGE OR YELLOW HANDS Leanna once had a shock when she saw a young woman with orange hands and thought she had been dyeing clothes. It transpired she had a new diet where she had to eat vast amounts of carrots! Her beta carotene levels must have gone through the roof.

COLD BLUE HANDS This is usually a sound indication the person has circulatory conditions or heart trouble.

WOODEN-LOOKING HANDS This is a strange thing to see and often present on hard-working, physical laborers. The hands are hard, bony, and dry.

YELLOW HANDS Could be linked to jaundice.

Psychic Palmistry Ritual

When a witch prepares for a palmistry reading, she will perform a ritual beforehand. The area where the reading is to take place will be smudged with white sage and a number of items will be placed on the table. Depending on what sort of witch you are, you might like to summon your preferred goddess or an angel or muse to assist you.

Materials

A white candle

A small wand

A white sage smudge stick

Crystals of your choosing

A small vase of fresh
  flowers of your choosing

A pentagram

Hand cream

A silver hand bell

A small flashlight

A large magnifying glass

RITUAL

Light a white candle and in your own words, ask your chosen deity to assist you with your client.

Holding the wand, smudge around the table a few times to purify it, and place any crystals you might like to use beside the candle.

Place a small vase of fresh flowers on your table, and a pentagram for protection. Sometimes your client will have very dry hands, so ask their permission to moisturize their hands with hand cream to make the lines more visible.

Ring a tiny hand bell over your client to dispel and negativity and cleanse their aura. Taking their hands in yours, hold them for a minute and try to tune into their vibration. Examine the backs of the hands, look at the nails, fingers and skin texture, using a flashlight and magnifying glass.

When you are tuned in, you should pick up whether your client is happy, excited or sad. Often, they can be very nervous, so be patient until they settle down making sure you keep good eye contact with them.

When the focus comes into the palm, take the little wand and point out the lines to the client, who will become enraptured with the mysteries that are to be revealed.

INITIALS AND IMAGES

Sometimes when we study the palm, we might be able to pick out letters or even images. It's never a good idea to ignore these as they can often have significance to the owner. Example, you might see the letter *A* on one of the lines or a *T* standing out somewhere on the hand. Always mention this and ask the querent if they have anyone in their life with these initials. Their mother might be named Anne or they could have a child named Tom. Images will work in the same way. You might see the faint outline of a bird or other creature and later find out that the querent has a passion for parrots.

GRID This looks like a block of tiny squares; or something like hashtag-type gridlines used for a game of tic-tac-toe. These represent difficulties and upsets. If you see these on the heart line, it could mean romantic upsets or on the lifeline hardship and obstacles. On the head line, mental issues, or health problems with ears, headaches, or dizziness.

PENTAGRAM A rare mark to see, it indicates that the person has magical powers to be unleashed in the future. It also represents spiritual protection.

CROSS A cross sometimes represents an accident, bad luck, or obstacles.
might even represent surgery, but where it is placed needs great skill to be sure of the outcome, so be careful how you handle mentioning it.

SQUARE If there is a cross on the hand with a square surrounding it (imagine a cross in a box), this can mean supreme protection. Generally, squares have two meanings, restrictions and protection.

STAR In Vedic palmistry, a star can be a spiritual sign for the owner, especially if it is placed in the center of the quadrangle (the space between the head and the heart line) but in traditional palmistry, it represents a recent shock or upset for the querent.

CIRCLE The West and the East have differing opinions on this. Vedic palmistry adherents think it's a good omen, Western palmistry the opposite.

Reading Initials—Leanna

I once saw the shape of a church and asked the female if she had just gotten married; she was amazed as the wedding was the month before. Another time the initial *T* appeared dramatically on the hand and the name Tim was given to me. The man sat opposite was stunned as his son Tim had died the year before and I was able to reassure him he was well and happy. By far the best was when I was methodically going over a young woman's palm, when a German Shepherd face appeared. I asked her about it and she informed me excitedly that she and her husband were going to pick up a puppy dog up at the end of the week.

BE PATIENT WITH YOURSELF

Because palmistry is a vast subject with many books written about it, the best thing to do is to get a sturdy folder or notebook to write everything down. Try to keep all of your notes in order. Fingers and nails for instance go together, as do the major lines.

Often, you will learn something and then forget it, but don't worry. Just concentrate on one topic a week until it sinks in. When I [Leanna] teach palmistry, I tell my students not to become overwhelmed with so much information and even I have to constantly look back at my portfolio of notes. When my mother started to teach me at quite a young age, I got resentful as it went straight in one ear and out the other. At one point she was about to give up but left me for a few months and we started again. So, remember it is normal for it all to become jumbled at times.

Chapter 8

Botanomancy: Psychic Plant Power

FOR THE GARDENERS AND OUTDOORSY TYPES AMONG us, there's nothing more natural than divining through the use of plants, herbs, bark, twigs, branches, seeds, or whatever can be found in the wild. Because there are so many types of plants, each with its own magickal energy, there are countless methods for incorporating nature into your psychic readings. This is an ancient practice known as *botanomancy*. A book on botany may be helpful if you are identifying plants for the first time.

In addition to talking about how to burn and use greenery and wildflowers to foretell the future, in this chapter we'll also discuss modern methods, such as aromatherapy, to prepare yourself so that you're in the right state of mind for the best reading possible.

BURN AND LEARN

Much of plant divination involves interpreting ashes. Certain plant and herb types were favored in ancient times—sycamore and fig leaves were thought to provide an abundance of good information, for instance— but you can use any leaves you have at hand. You can also use flowers that hold special meaning. Before you gather your flora to burn and interpret, consider these ideas and match them with what you are seeking in your answer:

Do you have dried flowers left over from a wedding, funeral, or special occasion? Might these yield interesting results? Is there a special tree, bush, or plant in your yard or that you see often with which you feel especially in tune? Have you always felt drawn to a particular fruit or herb?

When divining, consider the meanings and influences of certain flowers:

AMARYLLIS (*Hippaestrum*) Pride

AZALEA (*Rhododendron*) Gratitude

BABY'S-BREATH (*Gypsophila*) Innocence

BUTTERCUP (*Ranunculus L.*) Wealth

CARNATION, PINK (*Dianthus caryophyllus*) Motherly love

CARNATION, RED Passionate love

CARNATION, WHITE Purity and love

DAFFODIL (*Narcissus*) Fresh start

DAISY (*Bellis perennis*) Patience, innocence

IRIS Good news is coming

LILAC, PURPLE (*Syringa*) Love

LILAC, WHITE Memories

LILY, ORANGE (*Lilium*) Passion
(positive or negative)

LILY, WHITE Innocence, purity

LILY OF THE VALLEY (*Convallaria majalis*)
Humility, return of good times

MAGNOLIA (*Magnolia grandiflora*) Admiration
of nature

MORNING GLORY (*Ipomoea*) Unrequited love

NARCISSUS (*Amaryllidaceae*) Loving in
vain, ego

ORCHID (*Orchidaceae*) Ethereal beauty

PANSY (*Viola tricolor var. hortensis*) Loving
thoughts

PEONY (*Paeonia*) Shame, anger, shyness

POPPY, RED (*Papaver somniferum*)
Remembrance

POPPY, WHITE Peace

PRIMROSE (*Primula vulgaris*) Eternal adoration

ROSE, PINK (*Rosa*) Youth, friendship

ROSE, RED True love

ROSE, WHITE Innocence

SNOWDROP (*Galanthus*) Hope

SUNFLOWER (*Helianthus*) Purity

SWEET PEA (*Lathyrus odoratus*) Gratefulness

TULIP, RED (*Tulipa*) Eternal love

TULIP, WHITE Pointless love

TULIP, YELLOW Unrequited love

VIOLET, PURPLE (*Viola*) High aspirations
or dreams

VIOLET, WHITE Modesty

WISTERIA Homecoming or welcome

The meanings of these particular herbs and other greeneries should also be considered during divination:

BALSAM (*Impatiens*) Passionate love

BAMBOO (*Bambusoideae*) Strength, grace

CLOVE (*Syzygium aromaticum*) True, unending love

CORIANDER (*Coriandrum sativum*) Lust

FENNEL (*Foeniculum vulgare*) Strength

LAUREL (*Laurus nobilis*) Ambition, success

LAVENDER (*Lavandula*) Devotion

MINT (*Mentha*) Suspicion

OAK LEAVES (*Quercus*) Strength

ROSEMARY (*Rosmarinus officinalis*) Remembrance

THISTLE (*Cirsium vulgare*) Beware

WHEAT (*Triticum*) Prosperity

WILLOW (*Salix*) Love denied

Even fruit skins should be considered:

APPLE Temptation, lust, sin, suffering

GRAPE, GRAPEVINE Prosperity, fertility

KIWI Obstacles

MANGO Love, wealth, immortality

ORANGE Joy, prosperity

You can use the petals from a rose, the peel from an apple, a bundle of leaves, or the bark from oak tree—if it will burn, it's fair game! Before you strike the match, however, it's important to set your intention clearly. For example, if you want to know whether your current partner is "the one," then it is appropriate to burn a red rose. If you want to know how your job interview went, burn purple violets. If you're seeking information on whether a loved one will get well from their illness, burn snowdrops.

Whatever you burn, prepare accordingly. Prepare a quiet, peaceful space for your predictions so that you can concentrate on your intention. Like other forms of divination, try to make your question as clear as possible so that you will understand your reading. Consider how your ashy answers will be interpreted. The answer to a question such as "Which of my friends will be at my birthday party?" might be tough to decipher. But a question like "How many people will come to my party?"

or even "Show me what will happen at my party" might be easier to interpret, as they are likely to appear as numbers, a crowd, or some kind of event or activity.

A General Spell for Divining with Plants

The below spell can be used as a guide for your first divining ritual. **Note:** for your items to burn sufficiently, it's important to make sure that any flowers, leaves, or herbs you're going to burn are dried. A moist flower or plant may smolder and affect your results.

Materials

Your plant, flower, fruit peel or herb of choice, dried

Fireproof bowl, container, or surface

A lighter and some string or twine

Water, sand, or fire extinguisher, in case of emergencies

Ritual

Tie up your materials with some twine and place the bundle to be burned into your fireproof container. You may use several different types of materials to ensure a good burn and a readable answer.

Focus on your question. Take a moment to concentrate on what you want to know. Close your eyes and take several deep breaths, allowing your mind to open to the possibility of whatever the answer will be.

Using a lighter, light the bundle. Let it burn to ashes, watching carefully so that the flame doesn't get out of control.

When the leaves, petals, herbs, or fruit skins are ashes, it's time to read. Try not to stir the ashes with your breath or let the wind disturb them. What do you observe? Are there figures, numbers, or patterns in the ashes? Do they represent anything to you? If you're not sure of the general meaning of a particular symbol or figure, do some research on your own to find out.

AROMATHERAPY FOR CLEAR READINGS

Using plant-based essential oils can help accentuate your psychic abilities. Aromatherapy helps open the mind so you can access higher powers of knowledge and vision. Depending on the answers you're seeking or your current energy level, you may want to burn different oils or combinations of them. For example, mint is a stimulating scent, beneficial if your energy is lagging or you're having trouble finding answers to a question you seek. Orange, on the other hand, is a calming scent and may be helpful if you're particularly troubled about a question or topic.

Some oils to try and their uses are as follows:

BALSAM Intuition, grounding, eases stress

BASIL Clears the mind

BAY LEAF Insight, courage

BERGAMOT Calming, encourages optimism

CEDAR Strengthening, soothes anger

CHAMOMILE Acceptance, soothes irritability

CLARY SAGE Grounding, eases fear

CYPRESS Stabilizing, eases loss

EUCALYPTUS Stimulating

GERANIUM Safety and security

GRAPEFRUIT Promotes well-being

LAVENDER Calming, soothes anxiety

LEMON Concentration, stimulant

ROSEMARY Clarity

SAGE Meditative focus, eases anxiety

SANDALWOOD Bravery

TEA TREE Power, soothes anxiety and stress

VETIVER Grounding, clarity

YLANG-YLANG Optimism, soothes fears

You can use essential oils in several ways. You can put the oils in a bath, for instance, or use with a diffuser (either an electric one or a diffuser that uses a candle under a soapstone bowl). If you are going to use the oils on your skin, you must dilute them first, in a carrier oil like almond or coconut oil. The rule of thumb is 3–5 drops of essential oil per 1 teaspoon of carrier oil. Toss the solution when you are finished, as these preparations can become rancid quickly if not stored properly.

During use, allow the scent to fill your psychic workspace. Focus on your intention and allow your sixth sense to flow freely. Again, you can use oils in combination, so if you are seeking clarity on why you and your beloved recently broke up, for example, then you could try rosemary and cypress together.

DIVINING THROUGH
FRUIT, FLOWER, HERB, AND SEED

You can also use various fruits to divine the future. Here's a way to get an answer from an apple: Hold the apple by the stem with one hand while twisting it with the other hand. Recite the alphabet. The stem will come off the apple when you get to the letter of the first name of your true love. You can also use the apple seeds for this purpose. (You will need a candle in a container or a fire.) Assign the name of a possible love match to each of the seeds and toss them, one by one, into the flame. The seed that makes the loudest popping sound indicates the name of your future mate.

You can do something similar with watermelon seeds, by again assigning a love interest's name to each seed, then sticking each seed to your forehead. The one that falls off last is to be your future one and only.

Daisy petals are another way to know whether someone loves you. We've all done this one: Think of your love interest and then pick each petal off a daisy one at a time, saying, "They love me, they love me not." Continue until you've taken off all of the petals. The last petal will tell you if this a dream romance or a fly-by-night relationship!

Here's a little project that can help manifest an answer to a question with multiple possible answers: Take a handful of seeds and several small flowerpots. Label each pot with a possible answer or outcome. Plant seeds in each pot, all the while focusing on your intention or question. Care for each pot of seeds in exactly the same way. The pot that sprouts first (or, in the case of sprouts appearing at the same time, the pot that grows strongest) is your answer. You can try this outside, too, of course, especially if you're seeking an answer that has the potential to change over time!

Bay Watch

Bay leaves are especially useful in predicting the future, as they can be used in several ways. If you have a group of people present and you want to know, for example, who's going to get married first or who'll have the most successful new year, gather one bay leaf for each person present. With a pencil, mark one of the leaves with a dot or *X* on the back. Put the leaves in a pile, faceup, and have another friend write everyone's names on the leaves, as this person will have no idea which leaf has been marked. Now place the leaves in a bowl and have each person choose one leaf. The leaf with the mark on its back indicates the person who will get married first or have good fortune!

You can also give extra energy to your wishes by using bay leaves. Write your various dreams on several bay leaves and place them in a bowl to burn. This will underscore your intentions by sending them into the universe for manifestation! Bay leaves can also be burned during meditation or scrying to enhance metaphysical visions. *Dream pillows,* or pillows stuffed with bay leaves, can be used to augment visualizations as well.

Plants for Spells

Practitioners of magick take matters into their own hands by using brews and spells to bring their desires to fruition. Certain plants provide protection, boost your individual power, or enhance visions. You can start gathering some of these materials on your next walk in the outdoors. Of course, if you want to have an abundance of some of these plants, flowers, and herbs for use in your readings, you can plant your own psychic garden—a good idea if you're starting to do a lot of psychic work or if you are providing insights for friends and family!

ALOE (*Aloe vera*) Protects against evil spirits and mishaps at home

ANISE (*Pimpinella anisum*) Keeps nightmares away if placed in a pillow or sachet; keeps dark energies away when used during spellcasting or meditation

BASIL (*Ocimum basilicum*) Useful in love spells

BLACKBERRY (*Rubus*) Ensures good health and wards off evil spirits; also helps manifest money and success

BLACK COHOSH (*Actaea racemosa*) Another plant used in love spells; also promotes self-esteem, self-reliance, and self-assurance

BLOODROOT (*Sanguinaria*) **and CATNIP** (*Nepeta cataria*) Both attract love, peace, and positive energy to you; place on your nightstand with rose quartz

CHAMOMILE (*Matricaria chamomilla*) Brings money into your life and draws abundance in other areas of your life as well. Can also remove negative energies by soaking in it.

COWSLIP (*Primula veris*) Used in healing meditations and spells

ELDERBERRY (*Sambucus*) Promotes prosperity and removes negative energies; put it around your home—over doorways, on tables, or on your mantel— or carry a sprig with you

FENNEL (*Foeniculum vulgare*) Protects against dark energies; usually hung in windows and doorways or grown in the yard

HIBISCUS (*Hibiscus rosa-sinensis*) Brings love and abundance; useful in love spells

HOLLY (*Ilex*) Another plant used for protection from negative energies; also used in love spells and potions

LAVENDER (*Lavandula*) Useful in love spells—use lavender oil on your clothes or skin to attract someone into your life

MARIGOLD (*Tagetes*) Protects from negative energies and unwanted visitors; plant around the yard or keep inside your home

MINT (*Mentha*) Attracts success; protects from unwanted energies; draws positive spirits when used in a meditation or spell

NETTLE (*Urtica dioica*) Removes negative energies or reverses a curse; also used in healing

OAK (*Quercus*) Twigs and acorns, placed in and around the home, protect from storms, particularly lightning and floods

ROSE (*Rosa*) Popular for love spells; also attracts peace and well-being

Although you can find many time-tested spells in books and on the Internet, you can create your own spell or potion depending on your intention. Before you create a potion of any sort, however, make sure the herb or plant you're using is safe for human ingestion! And also consult your health-care practitioner first if you have any conditions

Are You a Hedge Witch?

The term *hedge witch* stems from ancient times, when people lived in villages near forests or woodlands. The forest or woodland perimeters were called "hedges." Because hedge witches have a love of all things nature-based, they use a variety of wild plants in their magickal rituals and are specialists in botanomancy. This type of witch tends to lean toward spiritual workings. Meditation, healing, and lucid dreaming are all part of their craft. In years gone by, the hedge witch would be the person you sought out for healing a minor ailment. They have a wide knowledge of medicinal herbs and plants and blend their own remedies by the light of the moon.

that might have interactions with ANY types of herbs or plants. Something like chamomile or mint is typically safe, of course, so let's say your intention is to have a more positive attitude and attract good things and people into your life. Opening up your meditative space while drinking a cup of mint tea is the perfect way to bring this about in your life. Sip the tea while you envision letting go of old sorrows and regrets, picturing the life and people you want. You can even chant an incantation if you want, something like,

> *"I picture the life that is to be,*
> *Spirits, please bring it to me."*

You can also make a potion or tea from blackberries while envisioning great success. Let's say you're an artist and you want to sell several of your pieces this year. Picture your artwork in great detail, imagine the person who will buy each piece, and envision the money you will receive in exchange. If you are looking for financial success in any sense of the term, you might use an incantation like,

> *"Money comes this way so free,*
> *This I know and this I see."*

Chapter 9

From Aeromancy to Tea Leaf Reading:
Other Forms of Divination

FROM EGYPT AND GREECE TO HINDUS AND HEBREWS, throughout time, each culture has had its own form of divination—the art of plugging into the universal life force to gain insight and knowledge. There are literally countless methods of divination, with most originating in ancient cultures. Centuries ago, folk interpreted cloud formations or read the dust on tables. They would look for answers by sacrificing roosters or by using a practice called carromancy or ceromancy, a divining method that studies all parts of a candle. Some divination techniques seem lost to time, but many witches sustained their practice through the centuries.

Here, we discuss the basics of some of the more common forms of divination not yet covered in this book: reading bones, studying markings on the body, observing the skies, candle reading, reading tea leaves, and salt reading. A list of more esoteric practices is included at the end of the chapter.

BONE TOSSING

Reading bones, or *osteomancy*, is a means of divination dating back to ancient China. In days of yore, Chinese seers consulted with the rich and powerful, whose questions varied from whether war or famine was coming to which spirit might be causing their ailments or had wiped out their livestock. In Asia, modern archeologists and historians have uncovered large quantities of turtle shells and singular animal bones engraved with cryptic writing.

Ancient diviners often used tortoise plastrons (the large belly covering) or the scapulas of oxen or other large animals for bone readings, as the relatively flat surfaces of these pieces made the job of question-and-answer a bit easier. The bones were cleaned of meat and then prepared with various tools to make their already-flat shape even flatter. Holes were drilled into the bones in a methodical fashion. The diviner would etch a question onto its surface. Then, using a rod or other means, heat was applied to a pit or a drilled hole until the bone cracked. The resulting pieces were interpreted by the diviner, and often the answer was etched in the bone afterward as well.

This method of bone divination differs slightly from the more modern practice you may be familiar with, which includes collecting a variety of bones, throwing them, and interpreting how they land. Casting bones in this manner is widely practiced today.

Where to Find Bones

Modern bone readers often use possum bones to connect with the spiritual plane and interpret its messages. Possums are believed to have a strong connection with the dead, as they are nocturnal animals sometimes seen roaming cemeteries in the dark. However, chickens have been used in sacrifices and rituals in African American hoodoo and African voodoo for many years, which indicates that this animal also has a powerful tie to the ancestral world. As chicken bones may be more readily available, they are a good choice for this form of divination.

Osteomancy is like many other methods of divination—it's highly personal. Standard osteomancy kits can be purchased online or from New Age shops, but while kits are a good start, it's preferable to use bones with which you have a personal connection. Some bone collectors say that using bones from roadkill gives them a stronger bond and better reading, as they:

- **Know where the bones came from**
- **Know something about how the animal died**
- **Can personally clean the bones**
- **Can honor the animal and give it a proper burial**

However, not everyone gets excited about the idea of harvesting bones from dead animals. So for those, like us, who tend to be a little squeamish, there are other options. Whether you buy them or find them, keep your bones together in a satchel or cloth. Add some additional objects that have personal significance to you, such as seashells, feathers, stones, pieces of bark, or even your own trinkets (keys, a loose earring, coins). This could be anything, as long as it's small enough to fit in the bag and toss with the bones, and as long as it holds special meaning.

Reading Bones

There are a couple of methods for bone reading, depending on which kind of bones you're using. If you purchase a kit and/or are using the mixed-bone method, it will include some standard pieces like a scapula, a tooth, a raccoon penile bone, and chicken wing bones. Other bones are included based on availability.

For example, they might represent:

PAST – FUTURE

PRESENT – OBSTACLES

Or, they may signify home, career, relationships, and health. Any other combination you come up with is suitable.

If you're using a plain cloth, decide before casting your stones how you will interpret their layout. Will objects that land closest to you be representative of current events, or will they speak to the past? Will you read the objects in a linear fashion at all, or will you read their layout as a big picture of events? Any bone or trinket that lands off of the cloth (or outside of your circular grid) will not be used in the reading at all.

Here's where your personal connection to the bones and other objects comes into play. Let's say you're using a bone that you found while walking in the woods. Before you found that bone, you were feeling melancholy, but after your discovery, you felt completely engaged with the nature around you. With this experience in mind, maybe that bone signifies redemption or rebirth for you. Before you start your reading, assign meaning to each object and bone in your collection so that you can interpret their presentation accordingly.

Keep a notebook of what the objects in your collection mean to you. Remember, this can be a fluid relationship: today, maybe an acorn indicates growth, but next year it might represent something entirely different for reasons that are unknown to you now. That is okay as long as you take the time to connect with your bone-throwing collection on a regular basis, to infuse it with your own energy.

Tossing Chicken Bones

Chicken bones have some standard meanings, according to old-time readers. It is perfectly fine to use the bones of a chicken that you have eaten for dinner. Boil the bird to get the remaining meat off and remove the bones you'll be using for divination. (You may want to soak them in dish soap for a few days to get all the grease off). Once they are cleaned, soak them in peroxide (not bleach, as this will break down the bones) for a day or two to brighten them. Remove and dry, and they are ready for use. Some people paint their bones; some use them as they are.

Note that only seven bones can be used from an entire hen. Their meanings are below:

BREASTBONE Love, relationships, artistic endeavors, and passion in life and love

LEG BONE, BROKEN Delays, hindrances, isolation, frustration

LEG BONE, WHOLE Land travel, potential realized, opening opportunities

NECKBONE Scarcity in resources, loss, anxiety, poor decisions

RIB BONE Restrictions, obstacles, difficulties to overcome

THIGH BONE Spirituality, emotional trials, ancestors, spiritual gifts

WING BONE, BROKEN Freedom curtailed, being stuck, delays

WING BONE, WHOLE Freedom, air travel, possibilities, future improvement

WISHBONE Hopes, aspirations, dreams coming true, luck

Toss your chicken bones and notice how they land in relation to one another. There are some shapes the bones will take that may clue you into messages:

DIAGONAL LINE Separation as it relates to the bones around it

HORIZONTAL LINE Represents feminine energy; indicates a negative response

HORSESHOE Represents luck, unless it's upside-down, which represents negative energy

PARALLEL TO ONE ANOTHER The energies are in agreement

T-**SHAPE** One bone is blocking the energy of the other

UPRIGHT TRIANGLE Growth in a positive direction

UPSIDE-DOWN TRIANGLE Diminishing energy or growth

VERTICAL LINE Represents masculine energy, indicates a positive response

X-**SHAPE** Working together or against one another

As with any kind of divination, practice makes perfect. You need to throw the bones regularly to understand the relationship of the bones to one another, as well as their connection to your mind and spirit.

DIVINING USING THE BODY

There are several means of reading characteristics of or on the human body. For instance, *moleomancy* is the practice of interpreting birthmarks and moles to determine a person's fate as well as their true personality. Though it has its roots in ancient times, this form of divination is rather rare these days.

Birthmarks are often given higher regard than moles, but the interpretation of either is often quite literal, depending on your source and beliefs. For example, a mole on the forehead may indicate high intelligence and an unusually high level of creativity. A mole on the calf may signal someone is destined to travel great distances. A birthmark on the hip may indicate trouble in the joints, and so on. (**Note:** If, during an examination of your own body for moles, you notice moles that are large, irregular in color, or asymmetrical, or that have changed over time, please consult with a dermatologist.)

Some other, less literal interpretation of moles:

ABDOMEN, LOWER Person will regularly fail to deliver on promises

ABDOMEN, UPPER Discomfort with appearance and/or personality

BACK, NEAR SPINAL COLUMN Truthfulness and sincerity, well-liked and popular

BACK, LEFT Daring, brave, determined

BACK, RIGHT Tact, discretion, peacekeeper

CALF, LEFT Extensive travel and worldwide connections

CALF, RIGHT Accomplishments, achievement, success

CHEEK, LEFT Egotism, aloofness, overconfidence

CHEEK, RIGHT Kindness, loyalty, duty

CHEST, CENTER Money troubles will plague this person

CHEST, LEFT Intelligence coupled with social anxiety

CHEST, RIGHT Person will have female children

CHIN, CENTER Hails from nobility or royalty and commands great respect

CHIN, LEFT No-nonsense communicator, wasteful spender

CHIN, RIGHT Logical, balanced, wise

FOOT, LEFT Poor marriage with family troubles

FOOT, RIGHT Good marriage, devoted to family and higher power

HAND, LEFT Tries hard but experiences many letdowns

HAND, RIGHT Fortitude, grit, determination

NOSE, CENTER Poor health

NOSE, LEFT Dishonest and decadent

NOSE, RIGHT Effortless earnings and wealth

PHILTRUM Higher-than-average sex drive

THIGH, LEFT Artistic expression and talent

THIGH, RIGHT Bravery, extensive travel

WRIST, RIGHT OR LEFT Financial hardships in youth that will turn around in middle age

According to some forms of astrology, the placement of moles and birthmarks on the body can tell you about the influence of the planets when the person was in their mother's womb. Markings on the left side of the body indicate that the planets were exerting a feminine influence; markings on the right side of the body tell of a male influence. The color of a mole adds another layer of classification. Black moles are bad luck, while virtually any other color denotes good fortune. (Your dermatologist may or may not agree.) Some witches believe that a mole in this life is a wound or mark from a previous life and that you can carry these scars on your body from one life to the next.

There are many websites devoted to mole interpretation, so if you don't see a specific marking noted in this chapter, don't fret. Chances are high that it is defined somewhere in cyberspace.

GET YOUR HEAD IN THE CLOUDS

Who doesn't love watching big puffy clouds make their way across a summer sky, or storm clouds rolling in on the horizon? Did you know there is a way to discern the future from weather observations? This is a form of divination called *aeromancy*, and it involves the interpretation of clouds, currents, and the cosmos. (Just the thing for those of us who walk around with our head in the proverbial clouds all the time.)

Aeromancy allows the reader to connect with information from a higher source. The most important factor, as with any form of divination, is having the ability to clear your mind and receive and interpret incoming messages. It's especially important with aeromancy, because an agitated or overloaded mind just won't be able to see images in the clouds.

In order to have a successful aeromancy session, choose a day when reading different cloud formations will be possible. While you can really do this during many forms of weather, it's going to be very difficult to read clouds if the sky is a sheet of overcast gray with no visible differentiation in cloud forms. Find a comfortable spot where you can recline or lie flat on your back. Try to choose a place where there isn't a lot of foot traffic or excessive noise. If headphones and white noise or relaxing music help you clear your mind, use them.

Start by meditating, perhaps by saying or thinking something like,

"I ask to be free from judgment.
I wish to enter into this session with an open state of mind,
an open heart, and creative insight.
I ask that this be granted to me."

Breathe deeply and get yourself into a state of relaxation. Focus on your question with your eyes closed.

Now open your eyes. Let the cloud forms appear as whatever your mind wants them to be: faces, letters, numbers, animals, otherworldly beings—there's no limit. Close your eyes again and meditate on how these images relate to your question. Repeat the exercise if you feel inclined. Once you feel an answer may have been reached, write down the images in a journal. Some of the images may not make sense to you immediately, but they may ring a bell in a day or two.

That's it. You've had time to relax and observe the beauty of nature, and hopefully you've received the information you were looking for along the way.

LIGHT UP YOUR FUTURE

Many people use candles in their commonplace daily routine, as aromatherapy, or as ambient light, while others plug into the spiritual side of flame by using candles as offerings or in remembrance of a loved one. You can also use candles in a couple of ways to foretell or even influence the future. Candle spells are commonplace in Wiccan traditions, and while we're going to focus on how to use candles for divination (*ceromancy*), there are many circumstances in which you just can't have one without the other.

Candle Colors

Depending on how you intend to use your candles and what information you hope to gather, you'll want to choose your color with intention. For example, for better insight on a particular day of the week:

SUNDAY Yellow

MONDAY White, silver, gray

TUESDAY Red, burgundy

WEDNESDAY Purple

THURSDAY Blue

FRIDAY Green

SATURDAY Black, purple

For divination into specific areas of inquiry:

WHITE Peace, truthfulness

GREEN Money, financial success

YELLOW Health, fertility, finances

LAVENDER, SILVER Paranormal (enhances psychic energy)

PINK Humanity, love, self-esteem, friendship

BLUE Fidelity

ORANGE Bringing plans to fruition

RED Love, sex, passionate relationships

WHITE and BLACK protection from and destruction of dark energies

Now that you've determined what candle color is appropriate, here's where spells, intention, and candle reading can work together. Let's say you have your eye on an attractive neighbor and you'd like to draw that person's romantic attention your way. Here's what to do:

1. **Choose a red or pink candle,** which represents your romantic interest.

2. **Write or carve the person's name and the date you'd like to be a couple** (say, two weeks from the current date) on the candle (or on the glass if it's in a container).

3. **Anoint the candle with vegetable oil or an essential oil** associated with the matter at hand. (For a list of essential oils and their meanings, see pages 164–65.)

4. **Now sit for a moment and imagine yourself with this person.** Picture yourself on your first date. Where are you? What's the weather like? If you're ordering a meal, what's on your plate? What kind of conversation are the two of you having? Focus all of your positive energy into this visualization.

5. **When you have the scene set in your mind** and you feel that it's absolutely going to happen, light your candle. You can say a few words like, *"As I have seen, so it shall be."*

6. **Allow your candle burn.*** To check on how your spell or intention is progressing, you can read the candle drippings.

(*Note: never leave a burning candle unattended! Use a short candle or tealight candle if you need to save time.)

Reading Candle Wax

If you have a freestanding (pillar, taper, round, or square) candle, you can interpret the way the wax is melting. This form of divination is a lot like tea-leaf reading: simply look for images in the wax. As the candle is actively burning, images may appear and then change completely, or images might persist or reappear. In the case of a romantic love divination, you might see a heart appear in the wax as it melts, or drippings from the candle may form to represent a house or a bride.

Maybe the wax drippings will take shape in the form of another woman or man, who might represent a rival for your affections. If you are using a candle enclosed in a container, you can read the drippings by using a bowl of cool or room-temperature water. (Make sure to use a bowl that is a different color than your wax drippings so that you can clearly see the images that form.) Simply drip some of the wax into the water and observe the shapes that show up.

As with all forms of divination, you may choose to read your results as single answers to certain questions or as part of a bigger-picture narrative.

More Candlelight Interpretations

In addition to using candle wax to peer into the future, you can also observe the way your candle burns as a whole. Studying this will help you determine whether your intentions are going to be successful or if your energy is being blocked. Let us take the same example from before, with the love interest being the focus of the divination inquiry, and imagine we're using a freestanding candle for interpretation.

- **The candle melts evenly, perhaps "opening up" into a flower shape.**

  Your intention will become reality. This is an indication of your positive energy being received and returned freely, without obstruction.

- **The wick gets buried in the wax and goes out.**

  Your intention is being blocked, either by negative energy or by someone's opposition to your wishes.

- **The entire candle melts down to one large puddle of wax.**

  This is ideal! This means your intention is working, and it also gives you one large wax dripping to interpret.

You can also read the flame itself, which is a skill called *pyromancy*. If the flame . . .

BURNS HIGH Your intention is backed and met with positive energy.

BURNS LOW Negative or oppositional energy is blocking your intention.

SPITS OR POPS Spirits are trying to connect with you regarding your intention.

FLICKERS EXCESSIVELY Spirits are present. Crackling or popping indicates they are trying to speak with you.

NOT EASILY EXTINGUISHED Spirits are still working with your intention. Let the flame burn a while longer.

Of course, it goes without saying that you should never leave a candle unattended and you should always use caution when working with fire. If you must leave before the candle melts completely, use a drop of water or a candle extinguisher to put the flame out. This is a sign of respect to the spirits gathered and working on your request. You can revisit the issue again using the same candle and the same technique of visualization and preparation.

READING TEA LEAVES

For centuries people across the globe have been downing cups of tea simply to gaze into the messy residue and see what their future holds. Although it might seem surprising, this method of divination can be astonishingly accurate. It may be hard to believe that your future could boil down to a handful of tea leaves at the bottom of a cup, but once you learn the knack of deciphering the patterns and symbols, you can unfold a wealth of knowledge.

How do Wiccans use tea leaves in everyday practice? The same way psychics use them, really—to get a peek at what's coming around the bend or to clarify issues that are going on right now. Many people who don't have the know-how tend to misinterpret the symbols at the bottom of a cup and get to thinking that they are doomed to a life of toil and woe, when quite the opposite is true.

The correct term for this method of divination, which can also be practiced with coffee grounds, is *tasseography* (also known as *tasseomancy* or *tassology*). The word comes from the French word *tasse* (cup), which in turn is derived from the Arabic *tassa*. It is believed that tea-leaf readings were first practiced in ancient China and the Middle East, then moved west to Europe along with tea culture before finally reaching the shores of North America.

For some time, tea-leaf readings in the United States were associated with trickery and even thievery. It wasn't until the nineteenth century, with the American Civil War raging, that tea-leaf readings became popular, particularly in the Southern states. Legend has it that soldiers on the way to battle would stop at one of the many plantations along the way to rest, feed their horses, and have a cup of tea, and sometimes a member of the household would offer to tell the soldier his fortune (usually with a positive spin).

Visions Are Brewing

To create visions in your own tea leaves, you have to start cooking. But don't worry; this isn't rocket science or even culinary school.

To begin with, you will need a pot. It doesn't have to be anything fancy, just as long as it boils water. You will also need a white or light-colored cup. This will ensure that you can clearly make out the patterns and images you see in the sediment. The size of the cup is not important, but its width is, as a wider cup bottom will make it easier to see the tea leaves.

Fill the pot with water, put it on the stove, and wait for it to boil. Some people like to use bottled water because they say it's purer. If you don't have this on hand, you can use tap water and bless the pot by saying these words three times:

"Cleansed and blessed are thee,
Water pure so mote it be."

Put about half a teaspoon of loose tea leaves in the bottom of the cup. Stir them around while you wait for the water to boil. At this stage, it's important to concentrate on the questions or issues that you want answers to, so focus as best you can and try not to let your mind wander.

When the water in your pot has reached the boiling point, pour it into the cup and stir it for a minute or so, still keeping your mind focused on your questions. Let the tea cool down to a comfortable temperature and then drink it. It's important not to gulp the tea—not only will this give you terrible gas, but you could burn your mouth in the process. Gently strain it through your lips so that you don't drink all of the leaves along with the liquid. (A spittoon nearby could be handy.) It's tricky but worth all the fuss in the end!

When there's just a small amount of liquid left in the bottom of the cup, it's time to stop. Take the cup and swirl the remaining liquid clockwise three times. Put your hand over the top of the cup so you can swoosh the last bit of liquid up the sides without spilling. Now you're ready to read.

Turn Over a New Leaf

Tea-leaf readers from all cultures base their readings on interpreting the shapes formed by the dregs of leaves. When reading the leaves, you are truly getting in touch with your inner self and your subconscious mind. It's very similar to reading the inkblot in a Rorschach test.

Look at the shape created by the leaves. What does it look like to you? Use your imagination to associate a word with it. The first word that comes to mind is very important.

Let's say you asked the teacup if you would be successful in your career. You might imagine that the tea leaves form a car or a train. Tea-leaf reading is similar to dream interpretation in that they both use symbols. However, the symbols can be interpreted differently because a dream can show movement. For example, in a dream, a parked vehicle would indicate a dead-end or stagnant situation . . . your subconscious mind may be telling you that you are in a dead-end job. But in tea-leaf reading, since the tea leaves are always stationary, you cannot differentiate between movement and non-movement. Most people who see a car associate it with movement, so the subconscious mind would interpret a vehicle symbol as "keep moving forward."

There is an endless number of words, images, and associations in tea-leaf reading, so here is a short and simple list to help you get started:

- **BIRDS** Good omens
- **CAT** Brief illness
- **CIRCLE** Success ahead
- **CLOVER** Good luck
- **DIAMOND** Expect money from an unexpected source

- **HEART** A reward is coming your way
- **HOUSE** Represents the self; if the house is in good repair, so are you
- **KEY** A new venture is coming
- **LEAF** A new lease on life
- **MOUNTAIN** An unfinished task is dogging you
- **NUMBERS** Indicated time in months, days, or years
- **SHARP OBJECT** Danger
- **SNAKE** Wisdom
- **SQUARE** Caution!
- **TRIANGLE** Good karma

There are dozens of images associated with specific fortunes, and because this subject warrants its own book, I can include only a few here. If you fancy studying this subject at more length, hop on the Internet and look up "tea-leaf reading symbols." This information is readily available to you.

Start your reading at the handle of the cup (the handle represents the person whose fortune is being read). This is your chance to interpret the shapes as you see fit.

- **Images to the right of the handle represent things that might take place in the future.** Example: The tea leaves form into the shape of a couple holding hands, so the querent might be soon embarking on a new relationship.

- **Images to the left represent things that have happened previously.** Example: You may observe the image of a plane, so the person might have just come back from a trip.

- **Shapes close to the handle are signs relating to the querent's present circumstance.** Example: You could see the shape of a sad face, which would symbolize the querent having battled with life for a period.

- **Images near the top third of the cup show events that will transpire right away.** Example: If you see something that resembles a dollar sign, it might mean unexpected money is coming the querent's way.

- **Shapes in the middle third of the vessel represent events that will occur soon.** Example: The leaves might give the appearance of a cat or a dog, so a pet might be giving cause for concern to the owner in the next week or so.

- **Images on the bottom of the cup usually indicate things that will arise in the coming months.** Example: You might view wings or clouds so you would predict that the querent will be guided by the spirit world.

Track Your Tea Leaves

Keep a tea-leaf diary on hand whenever you consult the mystical cup. Look at the formations in the leaves. If you see a picture that isn't listed anywhere in your references, meditate on the symbol and use your psychic abilities to find words to represent it. Write down your new findings in your diary so that you can use that interpretation again. Every time you read the oracle, do the same thing. Soon you will be able to combine certain pictures with upcoming events in your life. Within a short time, you'll be predicting your days and events with amazing accuracy!

SALT READINGS

Halomancy (or *alomancy*) is the art of reading the future with salt. Salt has a long history of being connected to magickal practices. In ancient times, it was scarce and precious, so it is no wonder that, over the centuries, the superstition of spilling salt was considered bad luck. The only way to counteract the ill fortune was to throw a little of it over your left shoulder, so as to blind the devil standing there.

Even today, ancient practices of using salt for purification, protection, and consecration are continued. For example, salt is used to cleanse crystals and energy fields. When you take a cleansing bath prior to a ritual, it's recommended that you toss in a handful of Epsom salts to draw negative energy from your aura. And many practitioners of all sorts of magick sprinkle salt in each corner of the room in which they are casting a spell or performing a ritual. This prevents negative energies from entering the space.

There are several ways to use salt to divine your future:

1. **Sprinkle salt on a flat surface, like a table, and then observe the images that form.** Ridges of salt indicate rough times ahead, while dips and waves in the salt represent obstacles to overcome. If the salt lands in a level pattern, it means that everything is going to be just fine.

2. **Casting salt into a fire is a type of pyromancy.** The idea is to read the images in the sparks created by the salt hitting the flames.

3. **Another type of salt reading is a little like reading tea leaves.** Create a salt solution (1 teaspoon of salt to 1 tablespoon of liquid should do the trick) and swirl it around a container. If you're using a salt-and-water solution, we recommend placing it in a teacup with a dark interior so that the images can be easily seen.

Set it aside and allow the liquid to evaporate, then study the salt left within. The images you see during halomancy are indicative of your immediate future, making it an easy, inexpensive, and quick way to see what's coming into your life!

Aleuromancy

The practice of using salt to read the future likely started with a different form of divination: aleuromancy, or the use of flour for fortune-telling. In this practice, dough is mixed and separated into balls. If salt is available, it's added to the mix. Sacred symbols are written on slips of paper, added into the dough balls, and baked, in the same way that we now bake fortune cookies. Querents seeking psychic guidance each choose one dough ball, and a diviner determines the person's future based on the size and shape of the dough ball in conjunction with the symbol baked inside.

MORE DIVINATIONS FROM A–Z

Those of you exploring new methods of divination—keep in mind that this subject is vast! We cannot list all practices that exist, but here are some that you might find of interest. Information on some of these more obscure practices is readily available online.

ACULTOMANCY Reading the swinging of a needle

ANTHOMANCY The art of reading flowers

ASTRAGALOMANCY Divination through tossing dice or small bones

AUSTROMANCY Interpretation of wind

BATRAQUOMANCY Also *batrachomancy*; interpreting the movement of frogs, newts, or toads

BELOMANCY Divination by balancing or throwing arrows, or by drawing them out of a container

BIBLIOMANCY Divination by use of books, especially the Bible

BOTANOMANCY Divination by burning herbs or the branches of trees

CAPNOMANCY Decoding the rising smoke from a fire

CAUSINOMANCY Seeking information by burning objects

CLIDOMANCY Divination by keys

CONCHOMANCY Fortune-telling using seashells

DACTYLIOMANCY Fortune-telling using rings

DENDROMANCY Divination by reading the branches and leaves of trees, usually oak or mistletoe

GASTROMANCY Interpreting the sounds of the belly

GELOSCOPY Interpretation of a person's laughter

HEPATOSCOPY Divination by examination of animal livers

HYPNOMANCY Divining through use of sleep

ICHNOMANCY Determining qualities or characteristics by reading footprints

LAMPADOMANCY Divination using an oil lamp or torch

LITHOMANCY Interpretation of precious stones, charms, or talismans

MARGARITOMANCY Reading the future through the use of pearls

METOPOSCOPY Reading forehead lines

NOMANCY Divination based on names

ODONTOMANCY Divination through deciphering the shape and structure of teeth

OINOMANCY Foretelling the future by the appearance of wine

ONYCHOMANCY Interpretation of the images that appear on the reflective surface of fingernails held up to the sun

OOMANCY Divination through use of eggs

ORNISCOPY Deciphering bird behavior, such as movements, flight patterns, and songs

PSYCHOMANCY Divination using spirits

SPODOMANCY Also *tephramancy*; divination by interpreting cinders, soot, or ashes

XYLOMANCY Divination through the interpretation of wood shape or texture, or how wood burns

ZYGOMANCY Divination through the use of weights

Chapter 10

Numerology

SOME PEOPLE SEE NUMBERS AND IMMEDIATELY GET nervous. They sweat, they tremble, and suddenly they're back in tenth-grade math class with their heads swirling, not grasping a single concept!

If this describes you, it would be perfectly understandable for you to avoid the field of numerology. However, it would also be unfortunate, since numerology is one of the easiest forms of divination to master. In fact, many Wiccans believe in a mystical "name-over" that involves changing your name and, by doing so, changing your destiny to reach a more spiritual path in life (see pages 208–12 on destiny numbers).

There are no complex formulas to calculate, no theorems to wrap your head around, and no written tests. How easy is this numbers game? With a person's name and birth date, you can unlock a wealth of information about them.

PYTHAGOREAN PASSION

Numerology has been around for a long time. Pythagoras, the famous ancient Greek mathematician, refined the system used today sometime around the sixth century BCE. Although little is known about Pythagoras, it is believed that he and his followers considered numbers and divination to be universally interconnected.

By using the alphabet as a guide, the Pythagorean system of numerology assigns meaning to numbers in order to predict the future and intuit information about a person's character.

According to legend, while Pythagoras was alive, there were those who believed that his theories were dangerous and others who dismissed his writing as the ramblings of a madman. Because of this, he swore his many students to secrecy. Eventually, intimidated by his critics, Pythagoras set sail for Egypt, where he studied with the Chaldeans and developed his numerological theories further before moving on to Italy to set up his own school of philosophy. It is believed that this is where his true brilliance in mathematics emerged, giving rise to his theories in geometry, which are still taught in schools around the world today.

Shawn's Story—Called to Calculate

When I sat in class in the seventh grade, like Pythagoras, I saw numbers in a totally different light. To me, they were vibrant and alive, jumping and dancing across the blackboard. It was as if the numbers were speaking to me, and each digit had its own secret story to tell.

I probably had the only seventh-grade math teacher who assigned a project requiring further research in the local library. I call that fate, for reasons that will become clear in a moment. Bundled up in my warmest clothes, I trudged two miles in a heavy snowstorm, silently wishing that I were out with my mates, tossing snowballs. Instead, I was headed to sit for hours in silence, reading books on mathematical theories.

When I walked into that imposing building, I headed straight to the librarian and asked her if she had any books on numbers. Maybe she saw something in my eyes that set me apart from the other kids who passed through those massive oak doors, or maybe she was psychic and saw something within me that led her to believe I was seeking a much deeper truth. I'll never know, but I recall her handing me an old, tattered book on numerology, which I took over to a desk to read. When I opened the book and looked inside, chills ran up and down my spine. The pages were filled with information about a discipline that was completely foreign to me, where numbers had personalities and vibrations!

I can't remember how long I sat at that desk devouring the information, but my life changed forever on that fateful snowy day. I was about to embark upon a journey that would lead me into the strange and mysterious world of numerology.

NAMES, NUMBERS, AND PERSONALITY

The ancient teachings of numerology tell us that a name is more than just a collection of letters. These letters hold the key to your future and your destiny, and they affect how others perceive you. It's very easy to unlock the secrets of this art. To begin with, you need just two vital pieces of information—your name and your birth date.

At its simplest, nine numbers are used to set up a numerology chart: 1, 2, 3, 4, 5, 6, 7, 8, and 9. Each of the letters in a person's name corresponds to a number that you can easily find in the chart below.

1	2	3	4	5	6	7	8	9
A	B	C	D	E	F	G	H	I
J	K	L	M	N	O	P	Q	R
S	T	U	V	W	X	Y	Z	

Let's suppose your name is SUSAN DOE. You find your name number by adding together all the numbers that correspond to the letters in your name until you reach a number from 1 to 9. Let's see what Susan Doe's name number comes out to be, using the chart.

S=1, U=3, S=1, A=1, N=5, D=4, O=6, E=5

1 + 3 + 1 + 1 + 5 + 4 + 6 + 5 = 26.

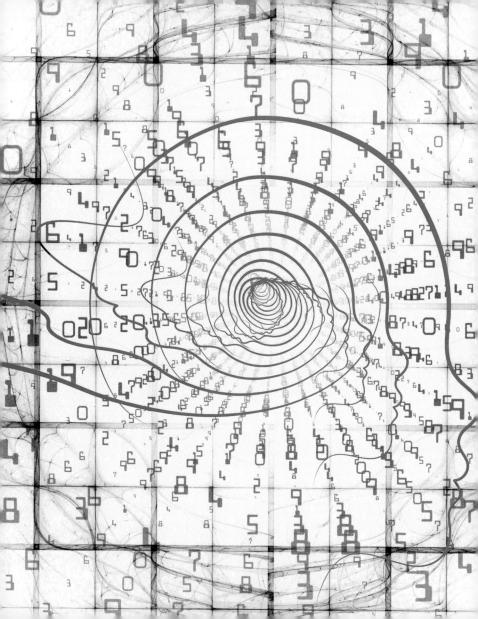

Now we reduce 26 to a single digit by adding the digits together: 2 + 6 = 8. Susan Doe's name now translates to a number 8, which denotes someone who possesses visionary powers and is highly intuitive.

Try this with your own name and see what your number says about your personality. The complete breakdown of numbers and their meanings is in the next section.

Your Personality Number

1: The Teacher

If your name number adds up to one, you are compassionate and sincere. You may feel the pain of others and want to reach out and help. You are not afraid of challenges and you're excellent at solving problems. Friends come to you with their troubles, seeking guidance and help. You are a deep thinker who teaches by example, so expect to spend a lot of time deep in thought. There is an imaginative and bright side to your nature, making you able to achieve anything you set your mind to.

On the negative side, you can be either extremely bossy or awfully shy, so try and find a balance somewhere in between. You may also have a tendency to leap before you look, so slow down and try not to be so impulsive.

2: The Nurturer

Twos see the best in everyone and are very tolerant when dealing with people's faults. You may feel that you have a kinship with those less fortunate than yourself, so you try to lift people's spirits by offering hope and optimism. Having two as your personal number means that you are wise, understanding, and sensitive. You have a harmonious aura that makes your personality magnetic. You are altruistic and nurturing, and you have leadership qualities that allow others to feed off your positivity.

At times you tend to hold back and not stick up for yourself. The lesson here is to try and become more assertive.

3: The Wise One

Threes are the first people friends and loved ones turn to for advice. Threes' innate wisdom is always dependable, always available. When presented with life's problems or challenges, you don't run a mile in the opposite direction; rather, you face them head on. Animals and nature play an important part in your life, and you will undoubtedly have a pet or two at some stage. You are charismatic, charming, positive, and determined. You are also gentle and wise beyond your years and have the ability to make everyone feel good.

Self-indulgence could be a problem, especially if you like your food and creature comforts. You also hate vigorous routine, so a monotonous job is not for you. Instead, you prefer a career that is changeable and imaginative.

4: The Seeker

Fours are quick wits! You have a tendency to look at everything under a finely tuned microscope and to be extremely analytical of others. Your earnest desire is to explore life and seek alternative roads to travel; you love to think up new ways of doing things. Like a three, you are a social creature and love being around people and animals. Stability and security are important in your life and you always aim to make everything harmonious around you. Like a star, you'll shine when you walk into a room, as others will find your communication skills captivating and interesting.

On a negative note, you could be a tad materialistic, paying more attention to possessions than you really should. Make an effort more often to share with others around you what you have.

5: The Magnet

If your name number makes you a five, you are one confident and self-assured person. You have a heightened sense of intuition, coupled with a talent for healing others with your touch or voice. You revel in daydreaming, allowing your thoughts to take you to distant places, but putting your thoughts into action is second nature too. You have the ability to start off with a dream, meet the challenges necessary to turn that dream into reality, and became a great success in life. Consistency and stability are all-important to you, but even so, your love of adventure and travel play a huge role in your life, so expect to be jetting off to interesting locales.

There is something secretly special about you that others are drawn to. Your magnetic personality is an asset that will serve you well in life, but because you can be restless at times and become easily bored, you need to be mentally challenged, learning new skills to keep you grounded and in tune with earthly matters.

6: The Realist

Oh, boy, are sixes strong-minded and assertive! You certainly stick to your guns when you know you are right, and you rarely back down. You are there for anyone who needs you and are generous with your time and money, but to cross you is a big mistake. If pushed too far, you tend to be unforgiving and you stand your ground. You're patient up to a point, but no fool either.

Balance and order are enormously important to you, so your home is tidy and clean. Quiet times are essential for your peace of mind, and you love to bury your nose in a good book and lock yourself away for an hour or two.

Failure is not a word in your vocabulary. If you are faced with a challenge, you tackle it with vigor. You take a realistic view when beginning new projects, and you have the energy needed to get them done, but you should try not to be too opinionated and try to understand that everyone has to go through life at their own pace.

7: The Visionary

Here we have an individual who is blessed with extraordinary abilities to see the future. You have excellent communication skills and delight in a career that involves interacting with others.

You have a tremendous potential to right life's wrongs, and you may get angry or irritated when things are out of your control. Being an idealist, you have to be careful not to shoulder everyone's burdens; otherwise, you'll burn yourself out. You are sensitive, caring, and steady on your feet, but you can be thrown off balance by negative vibrations. Ambitious to the hilt, you're not afraid to branch out and reach your goals.

The downside of a seven personality? You may be a bit of a loner and perhaps even perceived as being aloof. If this bothers you (some people like to cultivate an air of mystery, others don't), just flash your grin. Smiles always warm up other people.

8: The Prophet

You are a complicated and interesting creature. To begin with, you are born with a sixth sense, but you need to develop your psychic focus to receive any messages that the universe sends to you. You have a tremendous ability to see beyond what is written and interpret what is not seen by the human eye. The prophet personality is strong-willed and determined and feels a need to change the world. Not only do you have a deep understanding of other people's needs, you're a delicate flower yourself, requiring nurturing and love.

Your mind is like an airplane propeller always in motion, churning around new ideas, and this makes you a person who sets trends and fashions. Your faults? You may push people aside if they stand in the way of your goals.

9: The Analyst

Analytical nines have no time to be bored. For you, there just aren't enough hours in the day to get everything done! You have a practical and methodical nature and are loyal and sincere. You're quick to learn and always put your thoughts into action to create an orderly and productive life.

Your heart is so big that you care deeply for strangers as well as friends and family. This makes you wise and accepting of all people, even (or especially) accepting of their faults. Keep your wise head firmly screwed on, though, because at times you can be a little too trusting of people. Usually, your unbelievable insight into the minds of others will kick in when you need it most, so you shouldn't go wrong too often. Being open-minded and interested in many subjects, you're likely to have a wide knowledge of all things.

When low or unhappy, nines tend to give in to vices and bad habits. Beware of this inclination and guard against it.

Number Name Games

One of the most frequent questions heard in numerology is "What happens if I don't like my name?" The beauty of numerology is that it works with you and your name changes and variants. It's not like an arranged marriage where you don't get to choose your mate. Choose the name you're most comfortable with and work with those digits. For example, let's say that the name on your birth certificate is Kathleen White, but you've always been called Kate, and though you gave up your maiden name years and years ago, you've always felt more connected to the surname White than to your married name. So to find your personality number, go with "Kate White." Likewise, if you've changed your name from Mary to Songbird (or Morningstar or Sunshine, for that matter), work with the name you feel most connected to. That's who you are in your heart; that's who you are in the universe. **Note:** If you do not use your middle name regularly, you can leave it out of the formula.

Adding Up Your Fate: Your Destiny and You

Mastering your destiny number is another fascinating aspect of numerology. This number describes your strongest points and how to make your destiny work for you.

To find your destiny number, add the digits of the month, day, and year of your birth, using the same simple procedure you used to find your personality number. Let's say your birth date is 3/18/1984 and you want to find out what your physical and spiritual missions are on this life plane. Just add 3 + 1 + 8 + 1 + 9 + 8 + 4. This adds up to 34. Add those digits together to find your destiny number, like this: 3 + 4 = 7.

Now let's look at the breakdown below to see what destiny has in store for you:

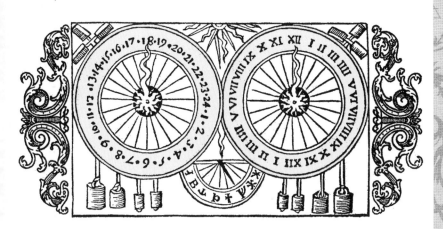

Destiny Number 1

You have phenomenal leadership skills that will come in handy when you're climbing the corporate ladder to success. Never let anyone sway your convictions or talk you out of believing in your dreams. Follow your intuition and the rewards will be great.

Destiny Number 2

You have boundless energy and are filled with optimism and enthusiasm. These skills will serve you well in life. Your mission is to guide people by your own example and help them find a new road if they become lost in their own dream world and doubt their role in life. It's important to remember that, be it through art, music, writing, or teaching, you have much to give others in life.

Destiny Number 3

You have an innate sense of other people's problems, and your mission is to help those who have doubts about their capabilities find their true inner light. This road can be demanding. It will require you to have empathy, understanding, and patience; however, since you are a natural caretaker, this task is a perfect fit for you.

Destiny Number 4

You are a very positive person who connects to other happy-go-lucky souls. However, be on the lookout for those who have faced personal tragedies and need your helping hand. Your purpose is to become a passionate believer in your inner power, You have the ability—by extending a helping hand with a calm and healing voice—to help people recycle negative thinking into productive thoughts that can heal their mind and spirit. Take advantage of every opportunity that comes your way. Don't be afraid to step outside your comfort zone and reach for the stars. By getting on the megaphone and not being afraid to speak your mind, you will be able to make a difference in another person's life. This could mean getting involved in politics or community affairs. There is a world out there waiting to be explored, and you are limited only by your imagination.

Destiny Number 5

You are blessed with strong willpower and the determination to succeed. These qualities will serve you well when you undertake new ventures or get involved in projects that can improve the quality of other people's lives. There will be times when you doubt yourself and feel the burdens of the world weighing heavily upon your shoulders, but keep trudging onward. The world is counting on you to realize your dreams!

Destiny Number 6

You are a great communicator—straightforward and honest. The world needs someone like you to tell it the truth. You are also an innovator and a motivator. With skills like these, you can succeed in politics or become a leader in community organizations that help people in need. You can also help save the planet by getting involved in "green" projects!

Destiny Number 7

You have the power and motivational qualities that inspire confidence in others. This suggests that you will go far in life, perhaps becoming a world leader or some other public figure. Certainly, the world is your oyster and you are the shining pearl that can light up the darkness in another person's life. Your true mission is to inspire, empower, and teach others to see beyond a stark black-and-white world.

Destiny Number 8

You have the visionary skills to see far into the future. You gravitate toward science, medicine, or writing, and you may make new discoveries or publish prophetic books. You will journey far and wide in your lifetime, unraveling the mysteries of life. You are also blessed with creative and communication skills, and you will use them to share your experiences with others, challenging them to reach for the stars!

Destiny Number 9

It is likely you will excel at anything in life that you want to do. You are detail-oriented, with leadership qualities that may allow you to walk among the giants in the corporate world. You're known as a mediator whose wisdom brings people of opposing views together. Your mission in life is twofold: to reach out to others and give them the confidence to succeed, and to encourage others to find the greater goodness within themselves.

BIRTHDAY SPELL MAGICK

You know you love your birthday. Even though your age creeps up, having your own special day never gets old.

Birthdays are also symbolically important. It is thought that the ritual of lighting candles started with a Greek tradition in honor of Artemis, goddess of the moon. Candles were placed on an altar, and if a person blew out all their birthday candles in one breath, then Artemis would grant their birthday wish.

Today, we still use this ancient tradition, although the altar has been replaced by a cake. While modern witches do participate in the birthday-cake-and-candle ceremony, we like to take it a step farther. For us, a birthday marks a very special event: it is the one time during the year when the universal energies are perfectly balanced for us and we can invite powerful magick into our lives with little effort.

How does this magick spell work? It's simple! Take the year you were born and add its digits together, reducing it to a single digit. Then do the same for the present year. Add these two numbers together and you'll come up with your life number for the present year. The nice thing about life numbers is that they cycle through the years from 1 to 9—every year brings its own little surprises.

If you were born in 1980, add $1 + 9 + 8 + 0 = 18$.

Then add $1 + 8 = 9$.

If the year is 2011, add $2 + 0 + 1 + 1 = 4$.

Add the two numbers together: $9 + 4 = 13$. Reduce to a single digit: $1 + 3 = 4$. Your life number in this example is four.

Once you have ascertained your life number, you can wait for your birthday to arrive, then cast a spell to enhance your life. As with most things magickal, life numbers correspond to different colors, so choose a candle in the appropriate color, listed on pages 214–18 for your future reference. In this example, your life number this year is one. This number corresponds to the color red and correlates to the Year of Discovery. To energize your candle, all you have to do is light it three feet away from something electrical, like your computer; you do not want to get too close as you want to avoid melting your laptop. Place a cup of water next to it. The candle will absorb the electrical energy coming from the appliance, adding to its magick and intensifying your life number for the year.

Let the candle burn for one hour (**do not leave unattended!**), then concentrate on your wish for a few minutes and blow the candle out. By this point, the water will be electrically charged, so when you have made your wish, wash your hands in the magickal water to seal the spell.

Candles, Colors, and the Year Ahead

As promised, here is a little peek at what you can expect in connection with your life number. What does this year hold in store for you?

1: The Year of Discovery
CANDLE COLOR: RED

This is a terrific year to explore new ideas and alternative ways of thinking. Relationships need some extra-special care, especially if you are critical or nitpicky with those you love. Adventure and rewards are in the cards, and you will receive lots of attention (and will more than likely enjoy great success) when starting new projects. Your creativity will know no bounds when you are reaching for a higher purpose in life, but be careful not to extend yourself so far that you become exhausted in trying to reach your dreams. The Year of Discovery brings many highlights, but you must dig deep to find the inner truth within yourself.

2: The Year of Enlightenment
CANDLE COLOR: YELLOW

Full steam ahead—don't look back and dwell on past failures; instead, look ahead to a year filled with endless possibilities. Lucky you! You'll certainly be busier than you have been in some time. This is an incredible year to fire up your inner spirit and put your thoughts into action.

If you're looking for relationships, look no farther than the end of your nose. The Perfect-Person-for-You could well be knocking at your door, so spruce yourself up and get a makeover. Career possibilities are also endless. Expect changes in the home or office, but don't push yourself too hard or you could run out of steam. You'll need to conserve your strength and energies to take on new projects, as many opportunities are just around the corner.

3: The Year of the Realist
CANDLE COLOR: WHITE

You are an unstoppable force this year! Valuable lessons can and will be learned, which in turn will prompt you to seek out new avenues of exploration. Although your feet are planted firmly on the ground, make sure your head doesn't get lost in the clouds. This is a very important year to stay grounded and focused.

Your best efforts will shine when you take on new projects, but don't be surprised if you feel your life is like a roller coaster. Part and parcel of being a realist is experiencing the ups and downs in life and learning from past mistakes.

4: The Year of the Wise One
CANDLE COLOR: BLUE

This year, burned bridges will be mended and new bridges will be built for you to explore. It is also a year when new doors of opportunity open up to you. Your life will take on exciting new dimensions as you grow, mature, and change. Marvelous adventures will take you to new lands filled with mystery.

This is the year to make changes and not be afraid to take risks. You may be a dreamer, but never underestimate the power of your dreams to come true! This year you could be faced with other people's problems; be prepared to lend a hand to those asking for help. Your guidance will assist others and you'll be offering advice to those in need.

5: The Year of the Truth Seeker
CANDLE COLOR: WHITE

This year everything finally seems clearer than it has in a long while! This is the time when you must consider what is right for you, so make a conscious effort to analyze your situation, starting with a spring cleaning for your life. (Out with the old—or with anything that just isn't serving you anymore.) The lesson here is to trust your inner feelings and separate yourself from people or situations that hinder your spirit.

If you play your cards right, career opportunities will abound! This is a potentially busy year with many unexpected events. Stay on your toes, but make sure you don't step on anyone else's little piggies in the pursuit of your goals. Love comes from strange and unusual places, and you could find your sweetheart literally standing next to you in the supermarket checkout line.

6: The Year of the Seeker
CANDLE COLOR: PINK

This year, you need to exercise a certain amount of restraint when faced with opposing views. You could do well in your career if you believe in yourself. You can rely on the strength of loved ones and friends, whose advice will see you through some tough situations.

Romance is in the air, and you just might meet your significant other if you're realistic in your expectations (so stop waiting for the latest heartthrob to call and give that guy in accounting a shot). Be prepared for unexpected changes in the home. If you are thinking of moving, this is a good year to start looking for that perfect property. Take care with your health and make sure that you are eating right, getting enough sleep, and not abusing your body. Self-indulgence will only deplete your energy this year and make you feel powerless.

7: The Year of the Dreamer
CANDLE COLOR: PURPLE

One of the most significant features of the Year of the Dreamer is prophetic dreaming—dreams that come true! You may start to take more of an interest in spiritual matters, so create a dream diary or learn the tarot.

New friends will be circulating in your orbit, and romance will tick along nicely. This is also the year when you can make radical changes in your lifestyle, such as going back to school, finding a new job, or going for a promotion. Your memory and concentration may not be at their best, so you could overlook or underestimate a potentially important event. Set realistic targets and focus on hitting them!

8: The Year of Empowerment
CANDLE COLOR: GOLD

This is the year when you will learn from your biggest mistakes. (Now, now, don't grumble—learning is *always* an opportunity!) It is also a time when your résumé needs some fine-tuning because of unexpected problems in the workplace.

Be assured that despite these challenges, things can and will work out for you as long as you continue to believe in yourself.

Family matters will also be in the spotlight, and you will be called upon to help someone in need. Animals will play an important role in the coming year, and you may take on a new pet or help an animal in distress. The Year of Empowerment is also significant when it comes to turning corners and meeting up with new responsibilities, all of which you can handle because you are resilient and have a reservoir of inner strength.

Your love life will be up and down, but be patient. You may not be content in love at the moment but . . . good things come to those who wait!

9: The Year of Contentment
CANDLE COLOR: GREEN

The 9 year is the completion of the numerological cycle, and it brings with it happiness and joy. (The best birthday gifts of all!) It's a time to plant the seeds for your future, keeping in mind that as you sow, so shall you reap. It is important that you keep your thoughts pure and positive, because your final destination is cosmic bliss.

One of your lessons this year is to break the monotony of having a closed mind and to become open to embracing new ideas. Career, home, love, and relationships take on a whole new meaning during this time in the life cycle; decisions made during this period will follow you as you go around the numerological wheel time and time again! Luck is on your side and everything you touch turns to gold. Share not only your time, but also your good fortune, and your karmic wheel will continue to turn in a positive way.

ANGELIC NUMEROLOGY

Angels have a unique form of communication for when they want to speak to us. Pythagoras said some variation of the credo, "Numbers rule the universe," and angels believe this to be true. So what is angelic numerology? Angelic numerology is quite simply a sequence of numbers you might see in your mind or dreams, or that, like an earworm with a song, might keep repeating over and over in your head. Celestial angels use a different form of language to gain your attention and deliver a message. Here, we list angelic numbers and their associated meanings, which will give you the opportunity to connect directly with your higher power for advice.

Who Is My Angel? A Little Bit of History

Let's talk about who our angels are. Judeo-Christian scripture tells us that angels have special powers and duties, and even have various ranks. Archangel Michael is one of the higher deities, having done battle with a dragon, while Gabriel is the angel who announced Jesus's impending birth. Raphael is the angel in charge of healing the sick. *Seraphim* are angel-like creatures stationed above God's throne, said to have six wings—although they only use two for flying. *Cherubim*, meanwhile, sit around the throne and praise God constantly.

Though angels are present in many religions, the term *guardian angel* is never used in the Bible. There are clues that imply, however, that these protectors are nearby, including, "For He shall give His angels charge over thee, to keep thee in all thy ways" (Psalm 91:11). So we know that beings watch over us, guide us, and can intervene in dangerous situations.

Many people believe that we all have a guardian angel assigned to us at birth, and this angel is with us throughout our entire lives.

Angels are not simply human spirits who have passed on to a nonphysical plane; they are immortal entities tasked with looking out for the welfare of all creatures on Earth. Wiccans believe guardian angels can provide you with guidance and wisdom when it's needed most. All you have to do is ask.

Here is an important distinction: although you may have a loved one in spirit who is nearby and might communicate with you, your angel plays a different role. Where your deceased grandmother may not be able to communicate with you telepathically, your angel can. Your angel can give you wisdom and guidance beyond your years and experience. We'll talk more about angel forms of communication toward the end of this chapter, but for now, just think about the differences between a mortal human and an ethereal, otherworldly creature, as well as what those differences mean in terms of the information they can offer.

Although angels have their roots in Abrahamic religions, nowadays many believers from every faith trust that they have an angel, or even numerous angels, guiding them. You don't have to be religious to have a helpful angel by your side; you can still be Wiccan or pagan and use angels in your spell craft. You merely need to believe in the many realms that we all inhabit and that the angelic beings are blessed with abilities that we can't even imagine! An open mind is key to learning.

Connect with Your Angels through Numbers

This is an easy way to make a direct connection with your angels and speak with them every day. You will need strips of paper in pieces just big enough to write a number on. You will also need a container to hold them in, such as a large jar, vase, or bowl. You may want to choose a pretty vessel that complements your interior style or work space aesthetic; you may be turning to it for many weeks, months, or years to come.

Cut one hundred little strips of paper. On each one, write the numbers one to one hundred. In the end, each piece of paper should have a number written on it. Place all the labeled paper strips into the container of your choice, whether it be jar, bowl, or shoebox. Keep your copy of *Psychic Spellcraft* close by for reference, with this section earmarked.

Whenever you feel you need guidance from an angel, or when you just want to connect with an otherworldly realm, reach into the bowl or jar and pull out one slip of paper. Before you choose a number, though, take a moment to say hello and ask for guidance. Although this can be a quick process, take the time to truly focus. You can simply close your eyes, bow your head, and say something like, "I ask you, my guardians, to guide me to the message you wish me to receive today. Help me understand whatever I am about to receive. Let me also be open to other messages from you during the day."

Now that your guardians know you're paying attention, reach in, swirl your hand around, and choose a slip of paper. Then pick up this book, open to the list below and on pages 223–30, and read the message associated with the number you pulled. When you are done, put the numbered slip back in with the others and mix them up again.

Here's what your angels are saying:

1. **Open your heart to someone who is difficult.** Take time to understand them and guide them wisely.

2. **Prepare for a change of scenery.** A new journey awaits you, so be brave and venture forward.

3. **Let go of an old grudge.** It is not right to harbor resentment. If you let it go, you will feel better.

4. **Put your inhibitions to one side and do something spontaneous.**

5. **Ask a loved one for help.** If you are feeling low in spirits, share your fears with another.

6. **Write an overdue letter.** Someone from your past misses you; you will make their day.

7. **Offer an apology.** Think about your actions in the past few months and put right any wrongdoing.

8. **Release your fears.** Conquer your weaknesses and you will not have to relive old lessons.

9. **Love is coming your way.** Someone new is to enter your life.

10. **Your prayer will be answered and your worries will soon pass.**

11. **Follow your instincts.** Listen to your inner voice, for I am speaking directly to your consciousness.

12. **The impossible is possible.** Take a chance and do something new.

13. **Acknowledge your strengths.** Your angel is proud of your accomplishments.

14. **A financial windfall is coming.** Don't worry; your finances will improve and all will be okay.

15. **Believe your dreams.** I speak to you in dream sleep, so pay attention.

16. **Your enemies will be silenced.** Have the strength to stand up to those who wish you ill.

17. **Family is your fortune.** Cherish your loved ones and wrap them in your heart.

18. **Keep your head held high.** You are stronger than you think.

19. **Ignore the critics and do the best you can.** You will achieve everything in the end.

20. **Protection is all around you.** You are never given anything you cannot cope with.

21. **Your health will improve.** Eat properly and sleep long and you will begin to feel better.

22. **You will have the patience to overcome adversity.** Trust in yourself.

23. **Kindness is never wasted.** Do a kind deed for someone else today and you will be rewarded.

24. **You are surrounded by love.** Your angels love you so much—remember that.

25. **Don't be afraid of change.** New beginnings are around the corner. This is your destiny.

26. **Be gentle with yourself.** Try not to be so self-critical. You are doing well.

27. **A new friend is coming.** Embrace new friendships and invite new people into your life.

28. **Your mistakes are forgiven.** Stop chastising yourself over past events.

29. **You have worked hard recently and your efforts will be rewarded.**

30. **Honor yourself.** Take time to meditate and listen to your inner thoughts.

31. **Let go of the past.** Think only about the future and the good you can do.

32. **An old friend is thinking of you.** Connect with someone from your past. Now is the time.

33. **Focus on a new dream.** Don't be frightened of trying new things. You will succeed.

34. **Be an example to others.** Fill your life with honesty and others will follow.

35. **Offer forgiveness to someone who isn't sorry.** They may be a younger soul than you.

36. **An unexpected event will occur in the next few days.** Deal with it wisely.

37. **What you believe to be true, is.** Trust your instincts.

38. **Focus on eating healthfully.** Food is fuel, so make sure to look after your body.

39. **Prepare for the past to repeat itself.** Old lessons will surface again.

40. **Even if it is just a few coins, donate to charity today.** Give a little and spread the fortune.

41. **Create harmony in your world.** Sit quietly and listen to peaceful music.

42. **A friend will bring joy to you.** A baby will be born soon.

43. **Tough times will turn around.** This long road of stress will soon come to an end.

44. **Try a new creative hobby.** It will make your soul sing.

45. **Take the time to listen to a family member.** They need your support.

46. **Count your blessings in life and cherish all your comforts.**

47. **Keep a cool head and try not to be angry with something or someone.**

48. **A child will excel in life through your input and guidance.**

49. **Release yourself from bad habits and start a new regime today.**

50. **Try to release all forms of jealousy; allow someone the freedom to follow their chosen path.**

51. **Love conquers all.** Gather the family together for a nice meal and share your experiences.

52. **Prepare for busy times; the next week is going to be demanding.**

53. **Pay extra attention to animals or pets.** They need you to ca[r]e for them.

54. **Share your insight with someone younger.** They will listen to you and remember your wisdom.

55. **You will change your residence in the future.** Living in a new home is your destiny.

56. **Ask the angels for what you want and we will help you achieve it.**

57. **Read some spiritual literature today and try** to **evolve your soul.**

58. **Learn from your errors.** Try not to repeat your past mistakes.

59. **Look at those around you.** Remove yourself from difficult individuals.

60. **Let go of sadness and think only of the happiness you can have in the future.**

61. **Offer support to someone today.** A kind action will help your soul develop.

62. **Express yourself to whoever needs to hear it.** Speak only the truth.

63. **Appreciate the beauty around you.** Take a walk in the outdoors.

64. **Embrace positivity.** Tomorrow will be a good day if you are in the right frame of mind.

65. **Ignore the naysayers in your life.** Move away from those who are negative.

66. **Don't let anxiety scare you.** Breathe in the essence of your angel when you are worried.

67. **Embrace the day and love your life!**

68. **Your loved ones are safe and protected in all that they do.**

69. **Expand your knowledge base.** Take on a new course or learn something new.

70. **Don't get involved in other people's quarrels.** Keep the middle line.

71. **Colleagues around you could be difficult.** Have patience with them.

72. **Someone you know might be going through a bad time.** Touch hands with them and try to help.

73. **Speak the truth always, but say it kindly.**

74. **Love your memories, but make room for the future.**

75. **Your guardians watch over you closely.** We love you and appreciate how hard you try in life.

76. **Believe you will succeed and you will.** Focus your mind.

77. **Rewards are coming to you.** You have saved up your luck and soon you will see sunshine again.

78. **Listen to someone who needs an ear.** Offloading their troubles will help them to see the situation clearly.

79. **It is never too late.** Do something you have always wanted to do.

80. **Choose wisely today.** Be careful when making decisions and listen to your heart.

81. **Do not put off actions until tomorrow!** Sort out anything that needs doing today.

82. **This world is your school.** Learn all that you can.

83. **Be generous with others.** Give items away that you no longer need.

84. **Treat yourself to something special.**

85. **Clear out your cupboards and create tidiness around you.** You will benefit from getting rid of clutter.

86. **Think about someone else today and make a difference in their life.**

87. **Be open to another's opinion.** They might not be right, but some truth will be spoken.

88. **Young people might be fractious, so have patience and listen to them.**

89. **Let yourself be happy today.** You deserve it.

90. **Relationships need more effort.** Spend time together and bring back the love.

91. **A journey by road awaits you.** I am guarding and protecting your heart.

92. **Spend more time sleeping and resting.** The future is going to be eventful.

93. **Do what you know to be right, and don't be misguided by others.**

94. **Simple joys are best.** Sit outdoors and watch the wildlife.

95. **Visit a neighbor or friend.** Your presence will put a smile on someone's face.

96. **Get back into baking and make a delicious treat for those around you.**

97. **Spend your money wisely.** Do not overspend on things you do not need.

98. **You cannot teach what you haven't learned.** Others will benefit from your past experiences.

99. **Cut down on unhealthy foods and limit your alcohol.**

100. **Plan a holiday.** You need to unwind and relax.

Combined Messages

Sometimes you may see a number or a sequence of numbers over and over again; many people identify 11:11 to be a significant time of day, for instance. Don't just ignore those instances when you notice them—something from the universe is at play. Combined messages can help make your communication with the angels more specifically.

If you feel that pulling more than one number maybe useful for you, or if you would like practice interpreting the message in multiple numbers, then feel free to pull two slips of paper from your jar.

Example: If you pull two slips of paper that number 76 and 92:

- **NUMBER 76 READS:** *Believe you will succeed and you will. Focus your mind.*

- **NUMBER 92 READS:** *Spend more time sleeping and resting. The future is going to be eventful.*

Your angelic message: Your future is going to be eventful, so you need to spend more time resting and sleeping. Focus your mind on self-belief and you will succeed.

Confusing Messages

With any kind of message coming from another plane, there can sometimes be a crossing of ethereal wires—or at least that's how *we* interpret it. Your angels are never wrong, of course, but they may sometimes be speaking about events that might not happen for some time or about distant event from your past that will relate to a future happening. Remember, time means nothing on the other side; it is just a construct that human beings use to organize events. If you are receiving messages that don't make sense you to right now, write them down. A whole series of events may take place before these messages come to fruition. Have faith. Just wait and see how it pans out.

Preparing to Receive

Picking a number from your jar is a nice way to get a quick daily message from your angels. Sometimes, though, you might want more impactful communication, especially when a particular problem has been plaguing you or when your worry runs deeper. In these cases it might help to meditate. This will open your mind to more in-depth information. Your meditation should focus on clearing the day's worries from your thoughts while simultaneously quieting any distractions. You can prepare your sacred space according to whether you have a specific question (appropriately colored candles, for instance) or whether you need some general guidance.

Many people choose to light a white candle when attempting to connect with their angels, as this color candle represents truth and peace. This will help draw your angel to your side and boost communication.

Some also choose to add a rose quartz stone, as this boosts positive energy. Quartz also helps clear the mind so you can receive and understand the messages coming through.

When your space is prepared and you are in a comfortable position, proceed as you would with any other meditation: Breathe deeply and close your eyes. Allow your mind to open and expand. Focus on your intention. Ask the questions that are on your mind, no matter what they are. And just let the answers come.

If you leave your session feeling as though you haven't received enough insight, know that our angels communicate in some very subtle ways, and not just when we call on them. For example, when you *just know* something is true or untrue, despite all other evidence to the contrary, that is because your angels are telling you it's so. When your intuition kicks in, often it's because your angels are leading you in a certain direction. When you see signs over and over again, guess who's responsible for either putting them in your path or opening your eyes to them? That's right—those busy, busy angels!

In fact, many abilities we consider psychic have some crossover with angel communication. Messages can come through in your dreams—and even your daydreams—so when you wake up with a premonition, you may have picked it up from another source: your angels whispering in your ear while you lay sleeping.

Also, when you are hit with sudden inspiration or an idea seems to come to you fully formed . . . that's a form of angelic communication. It's not to say that you aren't creative or clever; it's just that you have an extraordinary team helping you!

Do's and Don'ts

Angels are meant to guide you, not to make your life pitfall-free. In other words, even after you connect with them, there will still be some hard times and trials in your life. But it's during these times especially that you should call on them for help and guidance.

There's nothing necessarily off-limits when talking to your angel. If it's important to you, it's important to them. You can ask for safety (for you or loved ones), clarity, strength, wisdom, or intervention with the divine power on your behalf.

Some people call for guidance every day; others save their queries for major matters. There are folks who swear by calling on their angels when they are gardening, or people who speak to them about their loved ones' activities. Some people make it a practice to speak with their angels before getting out of bed in the morning or before they fall asleep at night. Others only communicate with their angels through numerology. You can do what feels right for you.

However, you might want to make a practice of "checking in" with your angel at least weekly, offering gratitude for their guidance and assistance. Remember that your angel is looking out for you and sending you numerology communications, whether you acknowledge it or not. It might be nice to say at least a quick hello and thank-you on a regular basis.

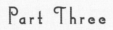

Part Three

DIVING
DEEPER

Chapter 11

Dreams and Astral Projection

DREAMS CAN BE MOST SIMPLY DESCRIBED AS SEQUENCES of images and sensations that we experience most often when we are in deep REM (rapid eye movement) sleep, which first occurs about ninety minutes after you fall sleep. Everyone dreams, even though you probably know some people who say, "I do *not* dream! I go to sleep and I wake up eight hours later without ever having one." The difference is that some of us remember our dreams in seemingly minute detail, while some of us recall absolutely nothing, for physiological and personality reasons scientists are just beginning to understand.

Regardless, most of us love a good night's sleep filled with all sorts of adventures and escapades. You probably know that you can use your dreams as a kind of mirror to understand what's bothering you in the daylight hours—but did you know that you can actually manipulate your dreams in order to visit different dimensions? The different dimensions one can visit are called "time warping." You can visit the past, present, or future. Sometimes you may even see "ghost lights" as we have seen numerous times when staying in haunted houses. For centuries, Wiccans have known the secret to making dreams come true—and it starts with controlling the dream itself.

DREAM TEAMS

In ancient Egypt, people believed that dreams were messages sent from the gods. These could be warnings of impending doom or harbingers of good things to come. The Egyptians were so fascinated by these nighttime dispatches that they created "dream books." Written on papyrus, the books were encyclopedias of dream symbols and interpretations. The ancient Egyptians also participated in the intriguing practice of "dream incubation": A person who needed guidance from a particular deity would visit the god's temple or shrine to take part in prayer and ritual, then sleep in the temple in order to receive a divine dream. In the morning, the petitioner would consult a priest about the images that had been incubated during the night, and the two of them would spend hours unraveling the messages in those symbols.

The writers of the Bible, too, recorded stories of people receiving revelations from God in their dreams, such as the passage in Genesis about Jacob, the grandson of Abraham and brother of Esau. While he was sleeping one night, Jacob dreamed of a ladder that reached all the way to heaven, from which God spoke to him.

In the sixteenth century, religious clerics theorized that if the devil appeared to you in dreams or if you had any impure dreams, then you must have the devil within you. Understandably, this idea sent lots of people into a panic; surely, if they had the devil within them, their nighttime visions were going to send them straight to hell!

Finally, in the nineteenth century, a French doctor named Alfred Maury formed many theories that laid the groundwork for modern-day dream interpretation. He hypothesized that external stimuli are the catalysts for dreams, including issues that confront us during our waking hours.

Dreaming the Future

According to sleep scientists, dreams are just a way for the subconscious to sort out some of the more confusing things that happen over the course of a typical day. This doesn't really seem logical when you're dreaming of climbing banana trees with a gang of monkey friends (unless, of course, this is what you do for fun during your waking hours), but that's where dream interpretation symbols can help. I'll give you the lowdown on these a little later in this chapter.

However, some dreams feel less like odd nighttime adventures and more like real life. And when you dream of something disturbing that's related to your daily life, it's worth taking a good, hard look at that dream. You could be getting a sneak peek at what's to come.

SUBCONSCIOUS REALITY

Who doesn't love a good dream? Whether you're sitting on a beach with a handsome man or a beautiful woman, strutting your stuff on a runway in Paris, or flying without the help of a jetpack, a great dream can feel like a real adventure, inspiring you and lifting your spirits all day long.

Bad dreams, on the other hand, can be totally disruptive. First, they can prevent you from getting a good night's sleep, which makes you cranky and less productive the following day. Second, the emotions associated with negative dreams can be very real. If you dream that your better half has dumped you or is having a wild affair, you might walk around the next day feeling genuinely despondent. This reaction is due in part to the fact that you are actually experiencing the emotions of the dream or empathizing with it in some way. Even though the events didn't happen during your waking hours, emotionally you have reacted in the same way you would have if those events really did happen. Most of the time these dreams stem from some deep-seated fear within you, but it could also be that you are having a premonition or a precognition that something upsetting is going to happen.

So let's look at the example of being dumped by your partner in a dream. Even though it hasn't really happened, it's worth exploring your subconscious to figure out why you had that dream in the first place. Is it possible that you:

- **Are insecure in your relationship and fear they may be bored with you?**
- **Think they're stepping out on you with someone else?**
- **Believe they're getting ready to break up with you?**
- **Are actually ready to move on without them but haven't admitted it to yourself yet?**

In cases like these, your dream may have handed you a vision of what's around the corner. Should you choose to accept this, then perhaps now is a good time to get to the bottom of it, probably by having a long conversation with your guy about what's really going on with the two of you.

This is not to say that all precognitions are bad. You might dream of a job promotion, winning a marathon, or becoming a famous actress, and find that in a short space of time you're on your way to success.

IN YOUR WILDEST DREAMS

Precognitions are neat little packages of the future that the universe delivers when we least expect it. However, there is a way we can control our dreams—and maybe even organize our future by creating positive visions.

Lucid dreaming is a way to remain consciously in control of your dreams. You tell your mind what's going to happen next; if the dream veers off into unacceptable territory, then you steer it back to where you want it. Usually, the dream starts off on its own—because you have to allow the subconscious mind some control. Once you become alert to the fact that it is a dream, you can then do whatever you feel like within it.

Some people use lucid dreams to prevent recurring nightmares; others use it to address self-esteem issues or to practice ways to handle a certain situation, anything from telling off a nosy neighbor to negotiating the purchase of a car. You can use this technique to dream up new spells and infuse them with your own spirit. Here's a step-by-step guide:

1. **Start by becoming more aware of your state of mind** in the days before attempting a lucid dream. Stop yourself every now and then

and say, "I'm awake. This is what's happening." You're just training your mind to recognize what is taking place at that moment.

2. **Before you go to bed, follow a soothing, relaxing bedtime routine.** Take a hot shower, put on comfortable nightclothes, and find your favorite blanket—whatever is going to allow you to drift off comfortably.

3. **When you lie down, concentrate on feeling yourself supported by the bed.** You want to relax every single part of your body. Breathe slowly and deeply.

4. **Now repeat to yourself, "I can control my dreams. I can control my dreams."** If you want to dream of something specific, try "I'm going to dream about _____."

Hopefully all this relaxation will allow you to slip right into your dream. When you begin the dreaming process, simply say to yourself, "I'm in charge here, and *this* is what's going to happen." Obviously, nothing is off limits, so make the most of it! Try out things you would never—or could never—do in your daytime life!

SLEEP YOUR WAY TO SUCCESS

We just explored how some people use lucid dreams to improve their self-esteem. Coaches and therapists have long advised their players and clients to use visualization to encourage successful outcomes. Visualization is really just a form of meditation, but since meditation is often described as a dreamlike state, it's fair game for our discussion here.

Let's say there's a house that you are desperate to buy. You're in a bidding war with two other potential buyers, and you just have to find a way to make it your own. Here's what to do to help ensure that you end up signing that deed:

1. **Prepare for meditation.** Sit or lie in a quiet room, free of distractions. Light incense, play some soothing music, and close your eyes.

2. **Breathe deeply**—in through the nose, out through the mouth.

3. **Feel every part of your body relax** and just give in to it.

4. **When you're as limp as a noodle,** start your visualization. View the house as though you're standing at the end of the driveway. Walk up the drive and unlock the front door with the key. Enter the house. Walk through each room, seeing your furniture and belongings as they will be when you live there. Sit on the couch. Kick your shoes off. Be in the moment in your new home.

When you open your eyes, congratulate yourself for closing the deal on the perfect place to live—be in the moment. That's yours to keep, but you have to make sure to store it correctly. Don't let doubt enter your mind; just know that things are going to work out in your favor; then behave that way in your dealings. We attract the same kind of energy we put out to the world; visualization just helps you to solidify that energy so it will be there when you need it.

DREAM JOURNALS

A really great way to enhance positive feelings from lucid dreaming and visualization is to keep a dream journal. Journals are also useful for keeping track of recurring dreams, especially those that are full of vague symbols you just can't make head or tail of. Journals can help you organize patterns of information and lead you to moments of discovery when you're able to say, "Oh, so *that's* why I'm dreaming about talking penguins!"

A dream journal can be any kind of notebook—the one caveat is that it has to fit on your nightstand. And you absolutely must keep a writing implement with it. You and I both know you aren't going to get up to search for a pencil when you wake up from a dream at three in the morning, and believe me, you will *not* remember the details of that dream when your alarm goes off at seven.

What Kind of Information Goes in the Journal?

The date, the time you went to bed, and anything significant—good, bad, or unusual—that happened during the day: these are the kinds of things you should note down before you hit the hay. Also, if you ate late at night or had something to eat that didn't sit well with you, include that too. Stomach upsets can wreak havoc on sleep and dream states, as can certain medications, so make a note of everything.

As soon as you wake up—whether it's in the middle of the night or in the morning—try to stay still. The less external stimulation you have, the better. Close your eyes and try to remember where your mind just came back from. If you're afraid you're going to fall back asleep and be late for work, before you go to bed be sure to set your alarm to go off a little earlier so you'll be able to hit the snooze button and take the time to retrace your dream steps. If you can grab on to any little detail of your dream, then go with it. Often one piece of information will lead you right back into your nighttime adventures. Stay in your unfocused state and go as far into recall as you can.

When you can't go any farther, open your eyes, grab your journal, and write. Don't worry about making a coherent story out of it, and don't worry about punctuation and spelling—just spit it all out. There will be time for analysis later.

You can also use a voice recorder to capture your initial impressions, but I think it's really important to have a written record of your dreams. It just makes it easier to recognize repetitive information and discern meaningful patterns.

DREAM SYMBOLS

Everybody dreams, even those who insist they don't, but everybody dreams differently. The reason is obvious: dreams are a reflection of the influences on the subconscious mind, and everybody has their own unique issues that manifest as nighttime nuttiness. But even though we all produce our own visions, there are some common recurring dream themes, like flying or standing naked in a crowd. What do these mean?

- **CEMETERIES** To dream of walking through a cemetery means that you are sad or fearful. But don't despair—it can also mean that you're on the verge of a rebirth of some sort!

- **FALLING** Falling with fear means you're feeling out of control or insecure. Enjoying the fall means that you're ready to take on new challenges.

- **FLYING** Flying is a reflection of your capabilities and suggests a sense of freedom. This means you know you can do it (whatever "it" is).

- **NAKEDNESS** Naked in public in your dream? You're feeling vulnerable.

- **STORMY WEATHER** Storm dreams indicate that you're feeling overwhelmed or angry.

- **TEETH** If your teeth are falling out in your dreams, it means you're feeling insecure romantically, you're worried about health issues, or you've been saying things you shouldn't during your waking hours. It can also be an omen of grave illness or even a death for someone you know.

- **TEST-TAKING** Taking a test means you're struggling with learning something or feeling insecure in your knowledge of something.

Now, when we get into talking about less common symbols, we could go on forever. There are entire books written about dream symbolism, so we're only going to discuss symbols that we feel are significant. If you don't find what you're looking for here, you can either do a simple Internet search ("dream symbols") or head to the library or bookstore to find a more complete listing.

See if any of these symbols speak to you in the dark of the night:

- **ABANDONMENT** Dreams where you're left behind mean that you need to let go of old beliefs and habits.

- **ACCIDENT** Dreaming of an accident is a reflection of an anxious state of mind. What are you worried about or scared of?

- **ADULTERY** If you dream you're cheating on your significant other, it could simply mean that you're mixed up in something unpleasant—but not necessarily an affair.

- **BASEMENTS** Going into a cellar in your dream indicates that you're suppressing some emotion or fear.

- **BEING CHASED** A dream where someone is hot on your tail means that you're unwilling to see another point of view on an important topic.

- **CELEBRATIONS AND PARTIES** If you dream of a party, you're achieving your goals.

- **CELEBRITIES** If celebrities are showing up in your dreams, it means that you will come into good luck soon.

- **DEATH** If you dream of your own death, you're going through a life transition.

- **FINDING SOMETHING** When you find something in your dream, it means that you're acknowledging part of yourself that you've been ignoring—maybe a newfound aspect of spirituality or a shift in your beliefs.

- **GARDEN** A garden of flowers indicates love and happiness in your life. A garden filled with weeds means that you need to clear your head regarding a spiritual issue.

- **KIDNAPPING** If you're being abducted in your dream, someone is exerting control over you—and you don't like it!

- **PREGNANCY** Being with child in your dream suggests not that you are actually pregnant, but that you're growing in some aspect of your life.

- **RESTROOMS** Dreaming of bathrooms means that you need more privacy in your daytime life (or it may mean you need to use the bathroom and your body is giving you a hint to wake you up).

- **RINGS** A ring in your dream is a good sign—it symbolizes loyalty and wholeness in your life. If the ring is broken, that's not so good. It means that someone is questioning your dedication.

- **RUNNING** If you're running from someone in your dream, you're really avoiding something in your life that you're afraid to face. If you are running toward something it means you are trying to reach a goal in your life.

- **WAR** Dreaming of war suggests that your waking hours are full of distress and chaos.

- **WATER** Water that is clear and smooth on the surface in your dream indicates peace of mind. Murky water suggests that negative emotions are nagging you.

This is just a partial list of dream symbols to get you started on dream interpretation. There are many dream symbol books on the market to help you learn more. I would suggest reserving a section of your dream journal for notes on symbols and what they mean. After you have a strange dream, look up the images and their meanings and write them down so that the next time they appear in your dreams, you won't have to hunt through pages of journal entries to find their meaning.

ASTRAL PROJECTION

One of the dream symbols just mentioned was death, but you'll notice we only talked about dreaming of your own death. When you dream of someone who has already died, there may be more to the picture than meets the "subconscious" eye. In fact, these may not be dreams at all. A person from the other side may have used astral projection to contact you.

Some people can develop a skill called astral projection, which is something like dreaming, in that the subconscious mind takes over— but in astral projection, your spirit actually leaves this earthly plane and enters into a different reality. Basically, astral projection is a way of releasing your spirit from your body and letting it fly free. Just watch out for birds and low-flying planes!

Astral projection can be used to visit loved ones on the other side, to relive moments you wish you could get back, or to gain knowledge from spirit guides. It may sound very supernatural and mysterious to you, but bear with me. This is another type of creative visualization, so even if you aren't completely sure that you want to leave this world and enter other dimensions, think of it as a way to open your mind and explore its limits.

To give astral projection a whirl, begin by following the same steps you would for meditation. Find a quiet spot, light candles, play music, burn incense, and breathe deeply. Then follow the steps below:

1. **Imagine a beam of white light shooting from your feet** right up through the top of your head. White light is always used for protection from sinister spirits or entities, and it will be important for this little journey you're about to take.

2. **Say a prayer for protection.**

3. **Imagine yourself tethered to your bed or to the ground** with a cord made of "white" or "pure" energy. Wiccans and psychics use what some might call white or pure energy to keep their souls attached to their bodies while in the dream state.

4. **Feel your spirit (or your soul or "second body," as some people call it) lift** and rise out of your physical body. Nothing can impede it—you can rise right through the ceiling, through the apartment above you, through the roof, and then go anywhere you want.

5. **If you encounter your spirit guides when you're out of your body,** go ahead and talk to them. Ask them anything you want—that's why you're in this state.

6. **If you feel scared, just remember that cord** that's keeping you bound to the physical plane. You can always simply say, "I want to go back now" and return to your body.

Some people experience a jolt or a sense of falling when they are just about to project. This may be because, as one theory puts it, the spirit doesn't gently float upward when it is leaving your body, but actually moves down into your back, out to the side, and then up. Have you ever been drifting off to sleep and then awakened with a start? This is when you know that you are on the brink of leaving your body.

Leanna has been experimenting with this for many years and is very skilled at astral projection, so she can go off at a moment's notice. She sees multicolored lights dancing behind her closed eyelids just before she goes on one of her travels. Once you get the hang of entering into this state, explore it. Talk to your spirit guides about the issues that concern you—your job, your family, how you're going to pay the rent next month, where you should go on vacation. There's nothing you can't do, nowhere you can't go, and nothing you can't ask! And since some spirit guides are thousands of years old, you may return home with information and advice you would never hear from anyone else. For more on spirit guides, see pages 272–76.

For more on spirit guides, see pages 272–76.

Sweet Astral Dreams

To make your dreams less chaotic and help your astral journey go smoothly, light a white candle an hour before bedtime and drink a cup of herbal tea (chamomile is a good one to try as it is known for its relaxing properties). When you have finished the tea, blow out the candle. This will heighten your vibration and cleanse your energies before you head off to the astral plane.

MAKE THE MOST OF DREAM TIME

Now that you have learned some neat little Wiccan dreaming tricks, we hope you'll never look at sleep the same way again. When you lie down at night, you aren't necessarily turning everything off until the sun comes back up—you can be sorting out your feelings, resolving confusion, and experiencing amazing adventures while your physical body takes some time out. So let your mind go and let your sleepy spirit fly free—you never know where you'll end up.

Chapter 12

Magickal Magnetism

THE PINEAL GLAND IS A TINY PINE CONE–SHAPED GLAND
that sits near the center of the brain, right where the two cerebral
hemispheres connect. Physiologically, the pineal gland regulates
reproductive hormones and produces melatonin, a hormone responsible
for our sleep-wake cycles. Too much light inhibits the release of
melatonin and disturbs your rest, which is why you might have trouble
falling asleep if you're on your phone or laptop right before bedtime.
Spiritually, though, the pineal gland has quite a rich history. The great
seventeenth-century French philosopher René Descartes was quite
firm in his belief that the pineal gland was the base of the soul and the
area of the brain responsible for all of our ideas.

Be it rumor, truth, or a legend passed down through the ages—because of its location in the center of the brain, which anatomically aligns with the center of the forehead, and its sensitivity to light—alternative medical practitioners refer to the pineal gland as the third eye (see pages 22 and 135). This chapter will discuss the use of magnetism to stimulate your third eye.

Magnets are at the very core of MRI (magnetic resonance imaging) machines. Your body has its own magnetic field, and treatments with magnets have become more common in alternative medicine and in some areas of Western medicine, such as psychiatry. Although the field is still being researched, alternative healers believe magnets can treat disorders ranging from insomnia to spinal disc hernias to high blood

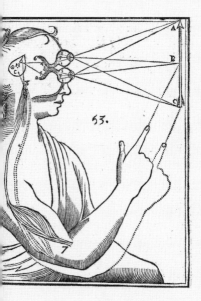

pressure, nausea, arthritis, gastrointestinal conditions, headaches, and even hemorrhoids. **Important note: Do NOT use magnets if you use a pacemaker, have an insulin pump, or are pregnant or breastfeeding. Also make sure to remove any magnets on your body before having an X-ray or getting an MRI. And as with all healing therapies, consult your health-care practitioner first.**

Some patients who have had an MRI have reported feeling more alert or having increased sensitivity to energies around them. One man we know who had an MRI after a car accident swears that he went from being an insensitive husband to be able to anticipate and deliver on his wife's needs—without her having to say a word! The change in his behavior was so dramatic that his wife suspected that the hospital must have sent the wrong husband back to her house!

NASA uses neodymium magnets to maintain the muscle tone of astronauts during space flights. Instead of offering patients with long-term depression electric convulsive therapy, a number of hospitals are moving toward transcranial magnetic stimulation to help alleviate symptoms. People seem to tolerate the treatments better with fewer serious side effects.

OPEN YOUR THIRD EYE WITH MAGNETS

To incorporate magnets into rituals to open your third eye, you DO NOT need to invest in expensive equipment! You can use any sort of magnet you have already in your home, or you can purchase magnets available in the office goods section of most big box stores or even your local grocery store!

You can also use magnetite, a stone with a natural magnetic field. Ancient Roman mythology has it that Magnes, a young shepherd, was walking through the countryside, wearing new sandals with unique iron pieces on the sole that was intended to improve traction. As he was searching for a wayward lamb, he felt his feet sticking to the earth. Looking down, he expected to find himself standing in mud or some sort of gummy substance, yet all he saw were stones beneath his sandals—and in fact, these stones were stuck to the iron pieces on the bottom of his sandals! Magnes had wandered into an area of a type of iron ore that would later be known as magnetite.

A lodestone is a particular form of magnetite with north-south polarity, and was used in early compasses. The word *lodestone* comes from Old English, and means "journey stone." Using lodestone in your ritual is a unique opportunity for you to find your way on your own mystical journey.

Magnetic Headwear

You can lie down in any comfortable spot and place a magnet or stone in the center of your forehead; however, the magnet may slip off if you fall asleep. You may also want to use a magnet while you sit in and meditate but holding it in place over your third eye will not be comfortable for more than a few minutes. To keep that magnet in place, make a third eye headband! You will need:

- **An elastic headband or sweatband**
- **Glue**
- **Beads, feathers, or other decorative baubles**
- **A plain magnet, either round or square, no more than 1 inch (2.5 cm) in diameter or circumference**

Simply glue the magnet to the headband. Use your decorative "extras" to accessorize and personalize your head wrap. You might choose the color of the headband to bring about your intention. For example, if you want to envision the love of your life, choose a red band. If you want to shed old worries and become pure of heart and mind, use a white band. A yellow band will help bring about a sense of peace and happiness. Buy a pack with multiple colors—one for each specific meditative purpose. Add two smaller magnets over the temple areas to enhance your psychic visions.

To keep your magnet centered on your third eye when you leave the house, you can attach it to the front (or inside the brim) of a hat with glue or strong tape. This might help those who want to find their inner peace while on a hike, nature walks, or even while relaxing on the beach.

Psychic Magnetic Dreaming

Here is an (almost) effortless way to enhance your psychic visions while you sleep. Before slipping off to dreamland:

1. **Put yourself into a tranquil state.**

2. **Start with a warm bath or shower** with lavender or vanilla bubbles.

3. **Imagine that you are washing away the day's stressors** and watching them vanish down the drain. Feel your muscles loosen in the warm water, focusing on releasing your neck, shoulders, and jaw—areas where we tend to carry tension.

Prepare your sleeping space for optimum dreaming. Write your questions on small slips of paper and place them under your pillow. Keep this simple so that you don't overwhelm yourself with racing thoughts.

Write down two or three (at the most) questions or intentions and state them as simply as possible. For example, "Will I find a new job?" or "Where should I go on vacation?" You can also place pictures (clippings from magazines, photos, or hand-drawn illustrations) under your pillow for an added boost.

Dress in your comfiest pajamas and climb into your bed, with an intention to clear your mind and allow dreams of clarity to come to you. Wear your magnetic headband overnight or place a magnet under your pillow. Better yet, invest in a magnetic pillow, which you can easily find online.

1. **Breathe in through the nose as deeply as you can;** hold for a beat, and then release the breath slowly through the mouth.

2. **Repeat, keeping your focus on your breathing.**

3. **As you start to feel more relaxed, bring to mind the topic** that you are seeking clarity on.

4. **Continue to focus on your breath as you set your intention for this vision.** You want to avoid making yourself anxious as you prepare for sleep. Remind yourself that you seek answers and that there will be time enough for worry in the morning when you are wide awake! Now is a time for peaceful contemplation and unlocking your third eye.

When you awake in the morning, take a moment to revisit and remember your dreams. Jot down the details in your dream journal before you start your day, as the details of those visions are often fleeting and difficult to recall later in the day.

Psychic Meditation with Magnets

The simple act of meditating has a myriad of health and spiritual benefits—lowered blood pressure, decreased pain and inflammation, improved sleep, and better mental health. Imagine how amazing you will feel if you meditate using magnets to help move gloomy energy out and bring positive energy!

To create a magnetic meditation zone, gather four magnets or lodestones. If you plan to lie down and meditate, place one magnet above your head and one below your feet and hold one in each hand. You can also use your magnetic pillow. If you are sitting, place a magnet at your feet, one in each hand and one at the top of your head (or use your magnetic headband).

Start your meditation, as always, by concentrating on your breath. (See chapter 2, pages 43–44, for instructions on beginning basic meditation.) As you begin to slip into a state of serenity and you feel your mind and heart expanding, allow your questions to come into focus. Again, keep it simple. There will be plenty of time to think in more detail later—for now, let just the basics come into play. In other words, try not to ask a compound question like, "What does my true love look like? Where will I meet this person? When will we get married? What will our house look like? Will we have children?"

Instead, pare it down to what this person looks like and where you will find them. During your next meditation, you can take it further. That's the beauty of meditating—the more you do it, the clearer the picture becomes, and by using your body's magnetic field, you can speed up the process!

Chapter 13

The Spirit World

MANY WITCHES BELIEVE IN AN AFTERLIFE, A PLACE where we go upon death and where souls can be crossed over with the help of their deceased family members or their spirit guides. One's final resting place is determined by the type of soul you have evolved into so you will only journey to the spirit plane that is likened to your nature. There are cases however when a soul is confused and might refuse to cross over. They can be anchored to a place where they once lived, or hang around living people they are familiar with. We call these spirits *ghosts*. Once in the spirit world, the deceased can communicate with the living by way of a medium if they choose.

Preparing: Self and Space

Prior to entering the psychic realm, you need to lay down a little protective groundwork. We are surrounded constantly by positive and negative energies, most of which exist in their own realms. It's important to keep it that way, especially when you start connecting with spirits on other planes.

We are all also surrounded by an aura, an energy field that belongs to us. This highly individualized atmosphere can be positive or negative, as it is a reflection of how we are feeling at the moment of perception. An aura can also act as a spiritual shield when cared for properly. Unfortunately, auras are easily affected by surrounding energies. In other words, if you are in a room with lots of negative people, your aura can absorb that energy and in turn affect your mood. But this only happens if you've inadvertently left an opening for that negative energy to enter.

The best way to secure against negative energies is through good defense, so you'll want to build a strong wall to block yourself and your aura from harm. Think of this as preparation for the emotional strain that psychic work can make on the body. Often, clairvoyants and mediums can experience a slight, dull ache across the bridge of the nose when psychically exhausted, so it is imperative that you recognize this, or any other sign particular to you, and see it as a signal to stop and rejuvenate your energy.

You wouldn't dream of running a marathon without preparing first, right? You must take your preparation for psychic work just as seriously in order to have the most positive experience possible.

Connecting with the Dead

If you feel you might have the gift of mediumship and want to sharpen your senses, it might help to know the following:

- **The deceased do not hang out in cemeteries.** They are usually found in places that held some meaning for them, like their homes, churches, favorite parks, etc.

- **It helps to connect with a deceased person if you have an article of clothing** or a personal effect of theirs. It is believed that their energy becomes imprinted on these objects, which allows the medium to gain access more easily.

- **People who die with some sort of unfinished business may be stuck between worlds,** which might make it easier for a medium to connect with them. Someone who died without warning may be reluctant to cross over to the next dimension.

- **Before conducting a medium session, or** *séance,* to connect with the dead, light a white candle and keep sea salt nearby. This will help protect from unwanted spirits entering the environment. Say an opening and closing prayer or statement of protection for the same reason.

- **Never work with entities that are unknown to you.** If you are hearing or sensing a spirit that feels the least bit dangerous, ask them to leave at once and end the session if you must.

- **Know that some spirits will be confused about where they are** and may believe they are still alive. Handling these situations requires a good deal of sensitivity on the part of the medium so as to not agitate an unstable spirit.

- **You can ask spirits whether they have any messages for their loved ones,** especially anyone who is present with you. The spirit may also sing a song that's familiar to their family or show a picture or symbol of something that their loved ones may be able to decipher.

- **It is vital to remember that all spirits were former humans,** and just as there are thousands of personality types in this world, there are as many on the other side. A kind person's spirit will live on in the astral realms, but wicked or vile individuals can also travel to the astral realm and might appear to a medium as a malevolent spirit. Always err on the side of caution and dismiss any spirit you are not comfortable with. It is all right to admit when you see or hear something you don't understand, but if you sense something downright scary, think twice before communicating it to the people around you. Ask yourself if this is necessary and helpful information or if it will cause distress.

A Ritual Bath to Cleanse Your Aura Eye

Your aura is your first line of defense against negative entities, so keeping it in a positive nature and bulletproof, so to speak, is essential. You can cleanse your aura with a simple bath.

Materials

Lavender essential oil, for relaxation and repairing the aura

Citrus essential oil (orange, lime, lemon), for recharging your aura

Bath salts, for detoxifying the mind and body

A white candle, scented or unscented

Ritual

Fill the tub with water that is a comfortable temperature for soaking. Add a handful of bath salts and several drops of both oils. Light the candle and place it where you will be able to see it. Soak in the bath for at least twenty minutes, clearing your mind of any negative thoughts or energy that may you have picked up during the day. Focus on breathing deeply, and imagine inhaling positive energy and forcefully exhaling negative energy. Let your eyes rest on the candle's flame while you envision a white light surrounding and protecting you. Use a washcloth or natural sponge to wash your body.

When your soak is complete, take care to stand in the tub and rinse yourself, either with the shower head or using a large cup and fresh water from the faucet. It's important to wash away any of the negative energy that may have emerged from your body while in the tub.

Dry yourself with a fresh towel and put on clean clothes (not the clothes you were wearing prior to your bath).

Once you're dry, dressed, and comfortable, take another moment to close your eyes and envision that white light of protection all around you—your newly cleansed and invigorated aura. When you feel strong in this vision, blow out the candle.

Crystal Field Recharging Ritual

You can also recharge and protect your aura by laying out crystals in a particular pattern. Choose from these precious gems:

- **BLACK TOURMALINE** Protects against negative energy
- **BLOODSTONE** Restores energy
- **CARNELIAN** Boosts creative thought
- **QUARTZ** Aids in clearing the mind
- **ROSE QUARTZ** Replaces negative energy with positive energy; boosts love vibrations
- **TURQUOISE** Aids in healing
- **AMETHYST, FIRE AGATE, FLUORITE, JET STONE, SMOKY QUARTZ, OR ANY DARK-COLORED STONE** Protects against and destroys negative energies

Materials

At least 1 protective stone for your crystal field and several others as needed, based on your specific intention

Ritual

Lay the stones on your bed or on your living room or bedroom floor. You can even practice this ritual outside.

Hold the stone that reflects the main objective for your psychic connection at this time. For example, if your main goal is to protect yourself from negative energies, hold an amethyst in your hand. If your goal is to find a creative way to connect with a spirit you haven't been able to speak with in previous psychic sessions, hold on to a carnelian. Lay the rest of the stones out in a pattern or circle that you can rest in the middle of. You can choose to sit in the center of the stones or lie flat.

Focus on your intention for this session. Envision it going just as planned with a successful outcome. When you are finished and feel ready for your reading, gather your crystals. You may employ the crystal used for your main intention (in this case the amethyst or carnelian) during your reading.

When you are finished with your reading, all of the crystals should soak overnight in a salt bath to cleanse them of any negative energy. Afterward set in sunlight or moonlight to recharge.

Smudge Your Space

Before you jump into any kind of psychic session, it's important to make sure the physical space you'll be working in is free from negative energies and entities. You can do this a couple of different ways.

The first method is to gather a bundle of dried sage (easily found at New Age shops or online). Sage has been used for thousands of years to clear spaces of bad energy and prepare them for positive forces.

Materials

Sand, to extinguish the sage after use

A fireproof container or bowl

Water, for safety

Matches or a lighter

A bundle of sage

Ritual

Fill your bowl with a moderate amount of sand, enough to easily tamp out the lit sage bundle like a cigarette. Have water or a fire extinguisher nearby in case of an emergency. Carefully light the sage over the bowl. You don't want the bundle to have an open flame for your cleansing ritual; blow out any active flame so that the bundle only produces smoke.

Fan the smoke with your hand to waft it around the space where you will be working. Move the bundle of sage up and down the length of your body to cleanse your aura.

As you smudge the area, include a prayer for protection and positive energy:

> *"I call upon the goddess to help cleanse and protect this*
> *space and to let in only the brightest of beings.*
> *So mote it be."*

You can also make up your own chant or incantation. This is to ensure that only well-meaning spirits or energies can access your space.

Put out the sage in the sand when you are finished. Take a moment to close your eyes and envision a positive connection during your divining session.

CONNECTING WITH THE COSMOS

Now that you have prepared yourself and your space, how do you go about connecting with spirits or gathering otherworldly information? One way (which might be the simplest for beginners) is by meditation— quieting your mind and freeing yourself from all of the distractions around you so that you can tune into more ethereal signals.

Choose a spot that is quiet and comfortable. Use a fan for white noise if you need to block out environmental noise. Make this space open to a positive energy flow; smudge it if you like, as described in the previous section. Light a candle or incense and dim the lights. If music will not be a distraction, play it at low volume.

Some meditation experts advise that you sit in a comfortable position. Lying flat is also all right, as long as you don't fall asleep. Breathe in as deeply through your nose as you can, and exhale as much as you can through your mouth. Repeat this, slowly, until you feel yourself starting to relax. It may be helpful to count your breaths—four beats in and four beats out, for instance. Focus on your breathing until it is all you are thinking about, continuing with deep inhalations and exhalations.

Now bring your question or goal to mind. Do you want to ask the spirits something? Or are you focusing on connecting with another entity? Allow your mind to travel in whatever direction it wants to go in search of information. Don't focus on whether it feels right or realistic; just continue to relax and go with the universal flow of the moment.

When you slowly bring yourself back to the present, write down your impressions. Were any of your senses heightened? Go through them, one by one: What did you hear, see, feel, taste, smell?

Practice this exercise as often as you can to make yourself more aware of your sixth sense. The more you practice this, the more it will become second nature and the easier it will be to access when you need it quickly.

SPIRIT GUIDES AND REINCARNATION: LEANNA'S STORY

From my earliest memory, I had an imaginary friend called Erik. I didn't set a place for him at the table or blame him for the small mishaps around the house. I never even saw him in his physical form. He visited me each night, just before I went to sleep, and his image would appear behind my closed eyes. He was blond with piercing blue eyes, and each time he arrived, I felt like I was being hugged, with huge, loving arms around me.

Erik was always the same age as me, and unlike most children whose imaginary friends disappear over time, mine didn't leave. He stayed with me throughout my childhood and on to adolescence.

I was three when Erik showed me my first vision. These revelations would always happen as I was drifting off to sleep. A few years later when I was eight, one night I saw a mental picture of my best friend at school falling from her bike and scraping all the skin off the right side of her face. Erik spoke to me and said not to get upset and that she would be all right, so I drifted into sleep, thinking nothing more of it. The next morning, I relayed the message to my mother over breakfast, describing in detail what I had seen and how my friend had blood all over her face. My mother was very good to me and never disputed what I said. A few days later, as Mother and I were waiting at the preschool gates, my friend arrived, and just as Erik had shown me, all the skin was scraped from the right side of her face. I stared at her, at which point her mum, who obviously thought I was distressed, said, "Don't worry Leanna, it looks worse than it is. She just took a tumble when she was riding her bike!"

As I grew older, so did Erik, and I would often dream of this young, fair-haired man, talking to me or giving me counsel whenever I was dealing with certain issues in life. It was only as I reached my teenage years that I realized he wasn't an imaginary friend at all—he was my spirit guide!

What Are Spirit Guides?

Spirit guides are souls, like us, that have reincarnated multiple times and over many thousands of years. During their incarnations, they will have dealt with almost every situation you can imagine and experienced all the human emotions that give us the knowledge and wisdom we need to evolve spiritually.

When a soul reincarnates repeatedly, it reaches a certain level of perfection, and although most guides are by no means perfect, there does come a point in the reincarnation process when they do not have to visit the earth plane anymore. This is because they simply can't learn anything new; instead, they are allocated individuals on Earth to guide and follow through their lives.

I have read many books that describe guides as being androgynous, but in my experiences, they have always had a gender. I have spoken about Erik, but in my twenties, I was also visited by a female in dream sleep, who I called Jane, mainly because she looks very similar to the actress Jane Seymour. She began appearing when I started having gynecological problems, so it seems that we may have guides who are specialized in certain fields.

About seven years ago, I found out I had another guide called Peter. This happened purely by chance. I am very lucky to have a stepfather who is a qualified, clinical hypnotherapist, and I had asked him for a past-life regression so that I could explore my previous lives. Some weeks later, he put me into a deep hypnosis and I traveled back to a time shortly before my birth in this life.

The feeling I had of being in the womb was strangely familiar to me and something I find hard to put into words. I experienced a slight ethereal sensation, like I was cocooned. Then he told me to travel back a little bit further, to a time before I was conceived.

As this happened, I was numb and felt totally detached from my body. I made my way through a dark tunnel, and up ahead were the brightest of lights. It didn't hurt my eyes to look—pure love was waiting for me in that light, and I knew I had to get to it as quickly as possible. When I finally arrived, the dark tunnel disappeared behind me until I was illuminated.

Standing in front of me were around twenty people. Some of the faces I remembered, and others I didn't recognize. My parents, my husband, and even my stepfather, who was sitting right next to me, were present in the group. Some of my dearest friends who I cherish in this life were assembled together, and everything was light and white and beautifully hazy. I felt quite emotional for a moment. It was a bit like going to a family reunion where everyone has their focus on you. We were all on the same vibration. Each of us was a little different from one another, but at the same time, I knew that we were all part of one another.

With each minute that I was under the hypnosis and quietly reflecting on the group, I came to understand that, without being told, you know absolutely everything when you die. You will instinctively know the answers to all of the questions you had as an earthly being. The people in front of me were members of my soul family, and as I studied my mother's face, I knew that we had reincarnated together many times before. I had a slight recollection that I had in fact been *her* mother in previous lives and that she had been my sister, cousin, and best friend in others. We had all reincarnated at some point with one another, swapping and changing roles. It was a very bizarre realization. I went on to recall snippets of each life as I quietly observed the group.

Then a figure stepped forward from the crowd and a man I have never met before in my earthly life was standing in front of me. I became very emotional and started to cry. I knew who he was: his name was Peter, and it felt like forever since I had seen him. How could I have forgotten him? Peter smiled and took my hands. It was incredibly strange, because my human brain knew that I had never met him before in my life, but my spiritual self recognized every single feature, from the color and shape of his eyes to the contour of his nose. I had an overwhelming love for him. It wasn't a romantic kind of love; it was much deeper than that. A more intense, safe, and secure love. He telepathically told me that he was my primary guide, and although he had always been there for me, he had taken over for Erik and Jane when I reached maturity.

In the years to come, I continued with my hypnotic regressions and traveled back to my "time between lives" on many occasions. I developed a thirst for knowledge. I needed to keep being reminded of what I already knew so that it could help me understand all the spiritual aspects of life and pass on the wisdom I have been allowed to enjoy.

I feel genuinely privileged to have a connection with my guide and even more fortunate to have been able to visit the spirit world during my hypnoses. I received so much information about the afterlife while I was there—too much to write down in a single chapter—but it has taught me so much, and for that, I am truly grateful.

What I Found Out About Reincarnation

During each hypnosis, I was instructed by my stepfather not to forget any of the information I had received during my visit between lives. Here are just some of the many findings I learned and remember.

Why do we reincarnate, and what's the point?

The entire point of reincarnation is so the soul can evolve. The more lives we have, the more we learn, and with that knowledge, our vibrational energy gradually raises.

We don't always return to Earth. There are many planets upon which we can be born. Earth is one of the more difficult places, where the lessons are harsher, but we can achieve so much more in a shorter time span when we choose to come here.

A the Creation of the Sun Moon & Stars

That word—*choose*—is key is my next recollection. We have a choice as to whether we reincarnate or not; no one forces us to be born. We sometimes feel the importance of reincarnation because we want to remain within our soul family. If our soulmates choose to return to Earth and we don't, then their soul will advance more quickly and they could potentially leave us behind.

How do our guides get messages to us?

When we have a niggling feeling about something—call it a hunch if you like—this is a sign that our guides are at work. They communicate with us through our emotions, so if you wake up one morning and have a sinking feeling about something, you must decipher it as a spiritual warning. We don't realize this, but our guides speak directly to us, at night when we sleep and throughout the day. Rather than us physically seeing or hearing them, they plant a seed in our minds that we interpret as our own thoughts or feelings. It's vital that we trust our instincts, because often it is our spirit friends making us feel a certain way.

The spirit world also sends us signs when certain things need to be done or when we need to take a particular direction in life. They can open the doors of opportunity, so if you get offered a job out of the blue, it is likely that your guide is presenting you with a new direction to take. I learned that it is vital to pay attention to everything going on around me in life and to always look at the bigger picture, for there is often a reason why things happen.

When our guides or loved ones in spirit want us to know they are nearby, they can sometimes send things called *apports*. These are small, solid objects, such as tiny crystals, pins, or keys that manifest from a nonphysical place. Items can be literally anything, but they usually have some significance to the receiver. Another item commonly sent from the spirit world is a single white feather. These represent angelic influence and often appear to a person when they need comfort. Feathers are also a sign of protection, so if you see a white feather in your path, you should know the angels are watching over you and that you are completely protected by the spirit world.

What happens when we die?

During one of my regressions, I went through the death process and was taken to the spirit world. Once I had traveled through the tunnel, I wasn't immediately transported to my final destination like I'd imagined I would be. I found that upon death, the soul first goes to a place comparable to a hospital, where spirit doctors work to cleanse and heal the soul before it can move on. Although there is said to be no such thing as time in the spirit world, this process can take a while, depending on how a person died. If it was a sudden death, the soul can be in a state of shock and will need time to acclimate to their new surroundings.

If a person has been very sick prior to death, they will need to have their soul balanced. Higher beings spend time with every person, aligning and purifying their soul, and it is only when this phase has been completed that you can move along to the next part of your journey.

Your guide usually assists you through the next transition, which is entering the spirit world. I was astonished at the true beauty of the spirit world; it was nothing like I could have ever imagined. Although it wasn't dissimilar to Earth, its splendor was enhanced a thousand times. Every detail of this euphoric place is heightened, each droplet of water is amplified, and the flowers sing in unison with the grass. I perceived colors that I have never seen before. I cannot even explain them to you. The mountains are soft pink and lavender in color, and there are even islands in the sky.

However, I eventually came to know that everyone's resting place is different. Because the spirit world knows every detail about you, your spiritual place is exactly in tune with your soul and will be exactly right for you. If you were a keen gardener in life, you might end up in the most beautiful garden with all your favorite plants and flowers. If you were a homebody, your spiritual place might be luxurious house catered to fit your exact needs.

Just before a person is scheduled to pass over from the place of transition to the spiritual world, their loved ones, already in spirit, get very excited. Imagine not seeing someone you love for a very long time.

The anticipation of being with them again sends a happy, frenzied feeling throughout the soul group. When you do finally reach them, you have a lot of catching up to do. If for some reason they weren't present at the welcome party, all you need to do is to mentally visualize the person you want to see, and within an instant they are right there with you.

Are we judged when we die?

Every situation we are faced with in life is watched and monitored from the spirit world. How we react to certain situations, the level of kindness we show in everyday life, and how we control our behavior is all paramount to our spiritual development.

Therefore, it is so important that while we are on this planet, we strive to be the best we can be. Each one of us has the ability to make a difference in this world and in the lives of others. No one person is greater than the other. We are all just as important as the next.

On my first journey, Peter took me to a large colonial-style building, where I was met by a group of beings dressed all in white. It was clear to me that they were there to assess the life I had just lived. It wasn't judgment day—far from it. It was simply a time when you are shown all the important events of your life so that you can understand where you achieved or failed in your mission. This can be an emotional time for the soul, but no one reprimands you if you didn't do something right; you are just made to see where you can improve next time. All this information is shown to you with a deep sense of love and understanding from these higher beings. You are also able to delve into the Akashic records (a compendium of all human events, thoughts, words, emotions, etc.) so you can be made aware of your past lives and compare your strengths or failings from then until now.

Only after this evaluation are you free to spend time in the spirit world with those you love. At least, until it is time to reincarnate again.

Is there such a thing as hell?

Your resting place is a reflection of your soul, so the more highly evolved you are, the more beautiful your place will be. Someone who is cruel or unkind or who has committed evil acts on the earth plane might find themselves in a darker place, one far less picturesque than the places given to those who apply themselves to doing good all through life. This place is not hell, but it's not pleasant, either. Whatever place you finally arrive at, you will be assisted by spirit helpers. These guides are proficient in encouraging young souls to reincarnate swiftly so that they can work their way out of this afterlife and strive toward something better.

The Three Key Stages of Spiritual Development

These are the three main categories, but there are hundreds of subcategories in between.

- **NOVICE SOUL** or young souls haven't reincarnated very much over the course of time. They can be selfish, narcissistic, aggressive, and abusive and can show cruelty, spite, or jealousy. Often, they do not show sympathy or compassion and can be cruel to animals or people.

- **INTERMEDIATE SOULS** have reincarnated many times and reached a certain level of spiritual understanding. They often have an interest in religion or faith. (It doesn't matter what religion or faith the beliefs fall into.) They are generally kind, caring, compassionate, and hardworking, have high morals, and show generosity. They have a long way to go as far as improving their spiritual status but are on the right track.

- **ADVANCED SOULS** have nearly fulfilled their reincarnation process on the earth plane. They have lived thousands of lives and have experienced nearly every human emotion possible. It is doubtful that you will meet many of these souls in life, as they are few and far between. They have a godly presence about them, are completely selfless, and have great understanding. They value the lives of others more than they value their own and will probably not have to return to the earth plane very much because they are already advancing rapidly. Once an advanced soul has completed their spiritual learning by way of reincarnation, they go on to be guides or will return as "Earth angels" to help a number of people with life problems.

Connecting with Your Spirit Guide

While under hypnosis, any doubt I had about the existence of a spirit world went straight from my mind. Every detail about the afterlife became clear to me. Having met Peter and, more importantly, being able to remember my time with him under hypnosis, I felt that I must learn to connect with him from my earthly bed.

Your guide will never want to frighten you, so it is unlikely that they will suddenly appear before your eyes in the cold light of day. To reach a successful connection, you must be prepared to experience a deeper level of consciousness. It can take a lot of practice to perfect, and only when you are at an advanced state in the meditative process can you begin to see visions. These will usually occur when you are in the middling stage between sleep and wakefulness or in the moments before you wake up. You might also want to keep a notepad and pen next to your bed, as it is common to be told relevant information in dream sleep.

Over the years and with a lot of practice, I have mastered the art of connection. For me, it's like looking at a screen, a bit like a video recording. The background is black and the images appear with gold edges. The pictures move like they would in a video and last anywhere between one and three minutes. Prior to the visions, I sometimes hear a ringing sound, a bit like tinnitus but not as annoying. This is when I know my soul is tuning into a higher frequency and I have finally connected.

Read on for simple tips and steps to help you achieve a connection with your spirit guide.

Items to have nearby

Crystals are very good to dot around the house, as they balance the energies in a room and can also help you to ground yourself. The following seven crystals help promote successful meditation. I recommend that you house these stones somewhere in the bedroom. Small, polished inexpensive versions, or tumble stones, work just as well as large, more-expensive pieces.

ANGELITE Used for summoning guides and angels

AMETHYST A calming stone used to enhance psychic ability and meditation

CLEAR QUARTZ Amplifies healing energy; the master healing stone

ROSE QUARTZ Relieves stress and tension; restores the aura by replacing negative energy with positive energy, boosts a love vibration

BLACK TOURMALINE A grounding stone that connects the Earth with the human spirit; aligns the chakras

AVENTURINE Energizes the Heart Chakra for wellbeing and calm emotions

CARNELIAN Improves concentration during meditation

Mindful meditation

Before embarking on any spirit communication, it is imperative that you mediate for at least thirty minutes. Lots of people find it hard to meditate for thirty minutes, but once you get the hang of it, it's very easy. Those of you who have researched meditation will know there are hundreds of ways to get into a meditative state. There is also a wealth of information online that can help you find the right method for you.

If you choose to perform your meditation during the waking hours, select a crystal and hold it in your hand. If you want to use all of them in your meditation, sit and space the stones in a circle around the base of the chair you're using or on the floor, should you choose to go without a chair. If you hope to meditate during your sleeping hours, situate the stone(s) either under the bed or next to wherever you are sleeping.

First, refer to chapter 2, pages 43–44, for steps on how to prepare for basic meditation.

1. **Concentrate on every part of your body, starting with your feet.** Relax the feet, focusing on each toe being completely floppy, then work up to the ankle, calf muscles, and so forth. Your aim is to be totally still, allowing yourself to become calm and tranquil. When you get to the area below the waist, hold a pelvic floor exercise for ten seconds, then clench your buttocks for a few seconds and relax. When you get to the top part of your body, raise your shoulders up toward your neck for five seconds before releasing them. You will feel a tingling sensation as they fall back to their usual position. Take your time. By the time you reach your facial muscles, you should be feeling extremely relaxed.

2. **Breathe steadily, either through your nose or mouth**—whichever is most comfortable. Take a deep, slow breath

inward and then exhale slowly. Repeat this for a few minutes or until you start to feel weightless. Clear your mind. Behind your closed eyes, focus on the darkness you see. See if you can pick out any shapes or lights.

3. **At this stage, you should be in a meditative state, so now is the time to ask your guides** for information. In your mind, ask your guide a series of questions, focusing on each question for a few minutes. Ask: *"I would like my guide to visit me. Are you there? Can you show yourself to me?"* You might see patterns and shapes behind your eyes or feel a strange sensation of belonging. The experience is different for everyone. If you don't feel anything, don't be disheartened. Remember, some guides will not show themselves to you while you are awake and might wait until a time when you are asleep. They know you better than you know yourself and may think that you are not ready to receive them in a conscious state. Then ask: *"Please show me your gender. Are you male, female, or nonbinary?"*

4. **Tune in psychically** and trust your inner thoughts and instincts. Imagine you are standing in front of a being. Tap into the energies and trust your very first answer. Ask: *"Can you tell me your name, please?"*

It might take several meditations before you receive this answer, but trust those instincts—you have them for a reason. Allow your imagination to expand. Your guide's name may not come quickly or even come to you at all when meditating. You might be given the name a few days later, so look out for signs. If, during the following days, you hear the same name repeatedly, perhaps on TV or on the radio, it could be your guide nudging you gently. Alternatively, you might wake up one morning with a clear name in your head.

Once you have your guide's name, you are on your way to connecting with them fully. If you are serious about making a connection with your guide, you must meditate every night before going to sleep. People often fall asleep during meditation; this is quite all right. When you arrive at a meditative state, your vibration rises and your energy starts to change and evolve. It does take lots of practice, so never give up. After a while you will be able to slip into this relaxed state quickly and summon your guide as needed.

Automatic Writing

Automatic writing, or psychography, as it is also known, is a way of psychically channeling your spirit guide to connect with you. This is a very good exercise to do straight after a meditation, because you need to be in a trance like state for it to work.

One of the best ways to get a positive result is to use pen and paper, although if you can type faster than you can write, you might find the computer to be a better option.

Sit at a table with your paper in front of you. Light a white candle to clear any negative energies in the room. If you are a beginner, it might be worth setting a fifteen-minute timer; short bursts of writing often give better results. Close your eyes or wear a blindfold. Ask your spirit helper to come through you and guide your hand.

Start writing on the paper. It doesn't matter what you are writing. You can start with your name and how you are feeling or you can just randomly write letters of the alphabet in some joined-up words. I usually start by writing my guide a letter, something like this: *"Dear Peter, please can you enter my subconscious today and guide my pen, sending me a message from the spirit world?"* (Don't be surprised if your writing resembles that of a six-year-old, either.)

You can also start by writing down or asking a question out loud. There may be something you want to know, such as whether you will get a new job soon, whether your children okay, if your health is going to improve. Good questions you might like to start with are as follows:

"What is your name?"
"Are you my guide?"
"Do I have a guardian angel?"
"Will my worries subside soon?"
"Will I get a new job?"
"Will I find a nice relationship?"

Literally write down anything at all you that desire to know. Write down or speak the question aloud, then concentrate on the pen and begin to write. You might start to feel your fingers tingling, or you may get a light-headed feeling. This happens when you have reached a connection with your guide.

Do not stop writing at any one time. Do not cross out or erase anything or worry about grammar or spelling. Try to get into the zone and feel the magick come from the pen, and continue to keep your eyes closed.

After around fifteen minutes of writing, open your eyes and read it back. Some of it might be garbled or make no sense at all. Don't worry too much about that. A word might not be spelled correctly, but you might be able to make out what it reads, or it could be in the form of an anagram:

olve = love,
or
Mynmaesiwillam = My name is William

When you become more experienced, you will psychically get into the zone and your messages will become clearer to read. Remember, practice makes perfect, so you should have a go at automatic writing every day. Just make sure the house is quiet and no one is going to disturb you.

DEMONS, DEVILS, AND MONSTERS

It is also important to understand that while tapping into this state of consciousness, we are also targets for darker energies, such as demonic beings.

Witches do not believe in the Devil because the term is a Christian concept, and Wicca practitioners do not believe in Christianity, but this doesn't mean malevolent entities are not out there. When we connect on an astral level, we can occasionally encounter a more disruptive soul who can appear to us as demonic, evil, or sinister. They are drawn to the purity of a more advanced soul, a bit like a moth to a light bulb, so it is vital that before you begin to tap into the other side, you know how to protect yourself.

Evil spirits thrive on our fear, which makes them stronger, so it is best not to give them a reaction, even if you feel scared or intimidated. These spirits often materialize when you are in the deepest of meditations; you might see an ugly face behind your closed eyes, or worse, attract something into the room with you. If this happens, you must summon the archangel Michael. Also ask your guides to protect you and surround you with a golden light.

The best way to deal with these kind of souls is to speak to them in terms they understand— basically, tell them to get lost. Show no fear and in no uncertain terms tell them that they are not welcome and to leave immediately. You will find that they just disappear before your eyes!

Prayer and Incantation for Protection

One of the ways you can stop them entering into your meditation is to perform a short ritual before you begin any kind of meditation.

Prepare with a Prayer

Lie in a comfortable position and imagine you are in a beautiful purple or golden bubble. For a few minutes, visualize a white light shining down upon your body. In your mind, say this prayer.

"I call upon all of the positive universal forces, my angels, my guides,
And my loved ones in spirit, to protect me during my connection.
Wrap me in your protective love and
Bring only the sweetest of souls to my being."

An Incantation for Evil Encounters

Memorize this chant for immediate use if you
have an unwanted visitor. Repeat these words
over and over until the evil spirit has gone:

> *"I call upon archangel Michael,*
> *healer and protector:*
> *Remove this entity from my face,*
> *Delete this image from my mind,*
> *Banish this evil through time and space,*
> *Bring only those that are pure and kind."*

The Rainbow Bridge

Many people who are spiritually inclined have a love of animals. We
cherish our pets, which often become our substitute children, and indulge
them in all manner of pampering, so it is no mistake that we regard them
as important members of our family. In some ways animals are more
significant than humans because they do not have a voice. While Leanna
was communicating with Peter some years ago, he informed her that
animals do not have any karma. Their purpose on Earth is to teach the
human soul compassion and to help us connect to a higher vibration.
By understanding the animal kingdom, and indeed by respecting every
creature, we elevate and purify our aura. Those who do not like animals
are probably younger souls that have not reincarnated very many times
(see pages 274, 277, and 279 on soul advancement).

When our animal friends die, the grief we feel can be just as
distressing as it is when losing a human member of the family. A

series of anonymous poems from the late twentieth century describes Rainbow Bridge, a place where animals are thought to go when they die—a beautiful, warm, outdoor place where our pets reside until it is our time to die. When we pass over, it is thought that our beloved pets become very excited at the prospect of meeting us again and will come greet us. We can spend time with them in the spirit world, reunited with our treasured companions.

If you're grieving a lost pet and the prospect of waiting until death to rejoin them seems unbearable, rest assured: animals who have passed over do come back to their owners from time to time. Here are the signs that they may have paid a visit:

1. **You dream of your pet.** When we sleep, our vibration is higher, so spirit people and animals find it easier to connect with us.

2. **Before dropping off to sleep,** you might feel like something is sitting on the bed, or you may experience a feeling of something heavy sleeping in your arms or nestled into your back.

3. **You feel something—your spirit cat or dog—**brush up against your leg when you least expect it.

4. **You hear a faint bark, or the cat flap will open on its own.**

And Finally . . .

Always be kind to yourself. You're not perfect, and that is the reason you're here. Everyone has a purpose in life, whether it be to overcome certain obstacles or to serve other people.

Never question "Why is this happening to me?" You have chosen this path for a reason, and however problematic or challenging your life is, you have agreed to experience it and will grow from the involvement and knowledge you acquire. Life is hard; it is a huge, global classroom where you come to learn difficult lessons. Look back on some of the toughest times in your life and ask yourself whether you would change what you have learned. If you hadn't undergone those hardships, you wouldn't be able to help or empathize with others who are going through something similar.

There are moments of joy in life; you must embrace them and keep them in your memories. But for now, understand that you are a part of the divine source that is seeking perfection, and this quest takes time—sometimes spanning many lifetimes. Never rush yourself or be false. Recognize your faults and practice being a better person. Invite a little spiritualism into your life every day, and give yourself time think and to reflect on why you are here.

Even when your insides are screaming, always try and be kind to others. A difficult child or a meddling mother-in-law might actually be a young soul you agreed to help. Try to be patient with everyone, for we are all going through life at different tempos. Remember, your spirit world might be different from someone else's, so to strive toward the beauty beyond, aim to be the very best that you can be—in this life and those to come.

Acknowledgments

We dreamed a dream of a brilliant editor, Barbara Berger, who would wave her magick pen and bring our words to life. We tip our wands and thank you, Barbara—for making our dreams come true. We dreamed another dream, an astute agent, Bill Gladstone, who believed in two witchlings from opposite sides of the pond whose magick transcended space and time. Thank you, Bill—for seeing into your crystal ball the future before us.

Also at Sterling, we are grateful to former cover art director Elizabeth Lindy for the stunning cover design, senior designer Shannon Plunkett for the beautiful interior design, project editors Ellina Litmanovich and Michael Cea, and production manager Ellen Hudson.

Picture Credits

Rijksmuseum: 63, 149

Shutterstock.com: agsandrew: 202; Airin.dizain: 92; Lopatin Anton: 134-136; ARTA DESIGN STUDIO: 91; Marijus Auruskevicius: 191; AVA Bitter: cover, i, 235 (raven); Robert Castillo: 35; chempina: 194; Croisy: 124; Danussa: 230; HikariD88: 108; intueri: 57, 126; Jan-ilu: 155; julia_janury: cover, spine, i (mirror); JuliaElfin: 128; Alenka Karabanova: 65; kuzmicheva: 278; Aleks Melnik: 31, 190; moopsi: 85 top; Morphart Creation: 66, 93; NataLima: cover, i, 59 (candle trio); nikiteev_konstantin: 186; Mila Okie: 282 (orb); Peratek: 130; Vera Petruk: endpapers, iii, 71, 77, 87, 107; pio3: 5, 131; Pixejoo: spine (moon in crystal); robin.ph: 121; Liliya Shlapak: 95, 267 left; standa_art: cover, throughout (art nouveau border); Bodor Tivadar: 79; vip2807: 127; WinWin artlab: v; Wonder-studio: 112-117; Vlada Young: 84, 109

Wellcome Library: 199, 238, 241, 255

Courtesy of Wikimedia Commons: 64, 119, 122, 153 top, 209, 228, 265, 266; Scott Freeman: 105; Metropolitan Museum of Art: 179

Index

Note: Page numbers in *italics* indicate specific spells/rituals.

A

Acultomancy, 196
Aeromancy (cloud interpretation), 181–83
Agate, 66, 83, 97, 268
Air element, cleansing pendulum, 137–38
Albite, 83, *93–94*
All-seeing, spell for, *102–4*
Aloe, 168
Alomancy (salt readings), 194–96
Alpha state, 21
Amaryllis, 159
Amblygonite, 83
Amethyst, 66, 83, 96–97, 125, 268–69, 284
Angelite, 284
Angels. *See also* Numerology, angelic
    beyond religion, 220–21
    do's and don'ts, 233
    guardian, 219–20
    loved ones in spirit distinguished from, 220
    who they are, historical perspective, 219–21
Animals, 291–92
Anise, 168
Anthomancy, 196
Apatite, 83

Apophyllite, 84
Apple, 162, 166
Aragonite, 84
Archangel Gabriel, 219
Archangel Michael, 219, 290, 291
Aromatherapy, 164–65
Astragalomancy, 196
Astral projection, *250–53*
Aura, rituals to cleanse and recharge, *267–69*
Austromancy, 196
Automatic writing, 287–89
Aventurine, 284
Azalea, 159
Azeztulite, 84
Azurite, *22–23*, 84

B

Baby's-breath, 159
Balsam, 161, 164
Bamboo, 161
Basil, 164, 168
Bath, ritual to cleanse aura eye, *267–68*
Baths, for crystals, 89–90
Batraquomancy, 196
Bay leaves, *94–95*, 164, 167
Bells, Tibetan, 91, 119
Belomancy, 196
Benitoite, 37, 84, *94–95*

Bergamot, 164
Beryl, 64, 84
Bible, psychic abilities and, 8–9, 237
Bibliomancy, 196
Birthday. *See* Numerology, birthday and
Birthmarks and moles, divining with, 179–81
Blackberry, 168, 171
Black cohosh, 168
Black tourmaline, 96–97, 105, 268–69, 284
Bloodroot, 168
Bloodstone, 84, 125, *268–69*
Blue agate, 66
Body, divining by interpreting birthmarks and moles (moleomancy), 179–81
Body language
    intuition and, 32–33
    reading, 52–55
Bone tossing. *See* Osteomancy
Botanomancy, 158–71. *See also* specific plants
    about: overview of, 158–59
    aromatherapy for clear readings, 164–65
    bay leaves especial use, 167
    burning and interpreting plants, 159–63

Botanomancy (*cont.*)
  defined, 158
  divining through flower, fruit, herb, and seed, 166–71
  general spell for divining with plants, *163–64*
  meanings, influences of specific flowers, 159–61
  meanings, influences of specific fruit skins, 162
  meanings, influences of specific herbs/greeneries, 161–62
  plants for spells (with properties), 168–69
Burning and interpreting plants, 159–63
Buttercup, 159

C
Calcite, 84, 126
Candles
  about: using in rituals, 91–92
  birthday spell magick, 212–18
  colors and their meanings, 184, 214–18
  divining with (ceromancy), 183–88
  interpreting burning patterns/characteristics, 187–88
  reading wax of, 186
  receiving angelic messages and, 231
  spell to attract romantic attention, *184–85*
Capnomancy, 196
Carnations, 159–60
Carnelian, *268–69*, 284
Causinomancy, 196

Cavansite, 84
Cayce, Edgar, 9
Cedar, 164
Chakra pendulums, 125
Chakras
  about: what they are and do, 133–36
  First (base or root), 134
  Second (sacral), 134
  Third (solar plexus), 134
  Fourth (heart), 134
  Fifth (throat), 135
  Sixth (brow or third eye), 135
  Seventh (crown), 135
  circular/oval grids around, 99–101
  crystals for, 83, 84, 284
  developing clairvoyance with your third eye, 22–23
  spell for strengthening psychic abilities, *93–94*
Chamomile, 164, 168, 253
Cheiro (William John Warner), 140
Cherubim, 219
Children
  exhibiting psychic abilities, 10–12
  reading palm lines of, 150–51
Chiromancy. *See* Palmistry
Chrysoberyl, 64, 85
Circle on hand, 155
Circular crystal grids, 99–101
Citrine, 66, 87, 90–91, 125
Clairalience, 12–13
Clairaudience, 6, 13, 23
Claircognizance, 13–14
Clairsentience, 6, 14, 20, 21
Clairvoyance
  alpha state and, 21
  availability to develop, 57

CIA Stargate Project and, 21
  crime solving and, 20–21
  defined, 6, 12
  developing with your third eye, 22–23
  enhancing powers of, 23
  exhaustion indicator, 263
  experience examples, 12
  historical examples, 9–10
  lapis lazuli and, 23
  misguided intuition and, 17
  a process of seeing explained, 19–20
  relaying difficult messages from, 17–19
  scryers and, 60
  seeing vs. *making*, 19
  Shawn's story, 15–21
  telling what you see, 19–20
Clary sage, 165
Cleansing and recharging
  crystal balls, 68–69
  crystals, 88–91
  pendulums, 137–38
  ritual bath to cleanse aura eye, 267–69
Clidomancy, 196
Closing ritual, 92
Clouds, interpreting (aeromancy), 181–83
Clove, 161
Clover, 192
Cognition, clear (claircognizance), 13–14
Color(s)
  candle, meaning and divination use, 184–85, 214–18
  of hands, palmistry and, 152–53
  in visions, indications of, 81

Communication
relaying difficult messages, 17–19
with spirits. *See*
Spirit guides and reincarnation; Spirit world
Computer, scrying with, 79–80
Conchomancy, 196
Connecting with spirit guide, 283–89
Coriander, 161
Covellite (Covelline), 85
Cowslip, 168
Crime, clairvoyance and solving, 20–21
Cross on hand, 155
Crowns, crystal, 96–97
Crystal balls
cleansing and storing, 68–69
connecting with/buying, 66–68
glass balls vs., 67–68
history of, 63–65
naming, 69
scrying with, 70–72 (*See also* Scrying)
Crystals. *See also* specific crystals
about: general characteristics, 82–83; "topping up" your stone, 92
characteristics for divination and psychic awareness (by stone), 83–87
cleansing and charging, 88–91
connecting with angels and, 232

connecting with spirit guide and, 284
empowering, 91
positioning and storing around home, 87–88
scrying and, 65–66
wearing, 104–5
Crystals, grids of, 95–104
about: functions and history of, 95–96
circles and ovals, 99–101
for crown, boosting inner vision, 96–97
dream enhancement with, 98
pyramids, 101–2
sleep mask to calm dreams, 99
spell for all-seeing, 102–4
spirals and stars, 101
Crystals, spells/rituals using
about: empowering crystals for, 91; general guidelines for, 91–92
for all-seeing, 102–4
crystal field (aura) recharging ritual, 268–69
heightening your instincts, 94–95
sleep mask to calm dreams, 99
strengthening psychic abilities, 93–94
Cypress, 165

D

Dactyliomancy, 197
Daffodil, 160
Daisy, 160, 166
Death. *See also* Spirit guides and reincarnation
about, 279–81

animals/pets and, 291–92
connecting with the dead. *See* Spirit world
hell and, 281
judgment after, 280–81
Delphic oracle, 8
Demons and devils, 289–91
Dendromancy, 197
Destiny numbers. *See* Numerology, birthday and
Devil, the
appearing in dreams, 238
Tarot card number 15, 114, 116
Wiccan and witches' view of, 38, 289
Divination, alphabetical guide, 196–97. *See also* Botanomancy; Candles; Crystals references; Osteomancy (bone tossing); Palmistry; Pendulum divining; Scrying; Tarot magick; Tea leaves, reading
Dreams
about: overview of, 236–37
angel communication and, 232
astral projection and, 250–53
bad, 239–40
controlling, lucid dreaming and, 241–44
crystals enhancing, 98–99
disturbed, crystal sleep mask for, 99
historical perspective, 237–38
intuition and, 33
keeping journal of, 33, 244–45

Dreams (cont.)
  making the most of, 253
  psychic magnetic dreaming,
    258–59
  remembering or not, 236
  seeing the future
    (precognitions), 239, 240
  subconscious reality,
    239–40
  symbols and their
    interpretations, 245–49
  "time warping" to visit
    different dimensions, 237
Dumortierite, 85

E

Earth element, cleansing
  pendulum, 137
Elderberry, 169
Elements, cleansing
  pendulums using, 137–38
Empathy, sixth sense. See
  Clairsentience
Empowering crystals, 91
Energy
  about: overview of, 2
  chakras and, 133–36
  dark (demons, devils,
    monsters), 289–91
  negative, crime solving and,
    20–21
  negative, crystals holding
    on to, 88
  negative, geodes
    neutralizing, 90
  negative, protecting
    yourself from, 263–71
  preparing for angel
    communication and,
    231–32
  tapping into to read
    vibration of another, 2

ESP. See also Intuition;
    Psychic abilities; specific
    abilities
  about: overview of, 10–12
  as catchall phrase, 39
  mediumship vs., 14–15
  not doubting, 48
  reading body language and,
    52–55
  seeing things vs. making
    things happen and, 19
  sharpening, exercise, 46–47
  testing, 48–50
Essential oils, aromatherapy
  with, 164–65
Eucalyptus, 165
Evil encounters. See
  Protection, prayer and
  incantation for

F

Fate line, 149–50
Fennel, 161, 169
Fingers and fingernails,
  143–45, 197. See also
  Palmistry
Fire agate, 268–69
Fire element, cleansing
  pendulum, 137
Five-card spread, 109
Flowers, divining with,
  159–63
Flowers, meanings and
  influences by type, 159–61
Fluorite, 85, 105, 125–26,
  268–69
Fruit skins, divining with,
  162–63

G

Gabriel (archangel), 219
Ganzfeld experiments, 62–63

Gastromancy, 197
Gazing, psychic. See Crystal
  balls; Mirrors; Scrying
Geloscopy, 197
Geranium, 165
Grapefruit, 165
Grape skins, 162
Grids, crystal. See Crystals,
  grids of
Grids on hand, 155

H

Hackmanite, 85
Halite, 85
Halomancy (salt readings),
  194–96
Hand size and shape, 141–43.
  See also Palmistry
Head line, 147–48
Headwear, magnetic,
  257–58
Hearing, sixth sense. See
  Clairaudience
Heart line, 146–47
Hedge witches, 170
Hematite, 66, 89, 105, 126
Hepatoscopy, 197
Herbs, divining with, 159–63
Herbs, meanings and
  influences by type, 161–62
Hibiscus, 169
History
  of bone tossing, 173–74
  of crystal balls, 63–65
  of dream interpretation,
    237–38
  of numerology, 199
  of pendulum divining, 122
  of psychics and seers, 7–10,
    172–73
  of scrying, 63–65
Holly, 169

Home, positioning crystals around, 87–88
Honey calcite, 126
Horseshoe spread, 109
Hypnomancy, 197

I
Ichnomancy, 197
Imagination, 45. *See also* Visualization
Instincts, heightening, *94–95*
Intuition
  about: overview of enhancing, 30–31
  analysis and/versus, 34
  asking questions and, 31–32
  body language and, 32–33
  dreams and, 33
  trusting, and tips for listening to, 34–37
  visualization exercise for, 31–32
Iolite, 85, 96–97
Iris, 160

J
Jeremejevite, 85
Jewelry, wearing crystals, 104–5
Judgment after death, 280–81

K
Kindness, importance of, 293
Kiwi skins, 162
Kyanite, *22–23*, 37, 85, 86, *102–4*, 105, 109

L
Labradorite, 85, 106
Lampadomancy, 197
Lapis lazuli, *22–23*, 23, 65, 85, 89, 126
Laurel, 161

Lavender, 96, 161, 165, 169, 184, *258–59*, *267–68*
Lemon, *94–95*, 165, *267–68*
Life line, 148–49
Life, perspective on, 293
Lilacs, 160
Lily of the valley, 160
Lilies, 160
Limonite. *See* Prophecy stone
Lithomancy, 197
Lucid dreaming, 170, *241–44*

M
Magick, magickal abilities, and practices
  automatic writing and, 288
  birthdays and numerology and, 212–14
  crystals and, 64, 82, 83, 88, 91, 102, 104
  full moon and, 90
  intuition and, 55
  Magickal Magnetism, 254–61
  mirrors and, 72–75
  plant energy and, 158, 168, 170
  salt and, 194, 195
  Tarot Magick, 106–19
Magnetite, 256–57
Magnets and magnetism, 254–61
  benefits of, 255–56
  headwear, 257–58
  magnetite and, 256–57
  MRI effects and, 255–56
  NASA using, 256
  opening third eye with, 256–59
  pineal gland, third eye and, 254–55
  psychic magnetic dreaming, *258–59*

  psychic meditation with magnets, 261
Magnolia, 160
Malachite, 66
"-mancy" divinations, alphabetical definitions, 196–97
Mango skins, 162
Margaritomancy, 197
Marigold, 169
Mask, crystal sleep, 99
Meditation
  "art" of, steps, 43–45
  automatic writing after, 287–89
  benefits of, 28, 44–45
  connecting with angels and, 231–32
  connecting with spirit guide, 283–87
  connecting with spirit world, 271–72
  crystals and, 125, 284
  developing clairvoyance with your third eye, 22–23
  dreams, visualization and, 242–44
  magnets and, 257–58, 261
  mindful, 284–87
  plants and, 165, 167, 168, 169
  prayer and incantation for protection, 290–92
  for reading clouds, 182–83
  scrying as, 63 (*See also* Scrying)
Mediumship
  about, 14–15
  connecting with the dead and, 264–65
  medium fingers and, 143

Merkaba (star-shaped)
pendulums, 124
Metoposcopy, 197
Michael (archangel), 219,
290, 291
Mint, 96, 161, 164, 169, 171
Mirrors
black (obsidian) mirror
scrying, 74–77
divination using, 72–77
in fairy tales/mystical
stories, 72–73
soul reflection and, 73
uses in magick, 74–75
Moldavite, 85
Moleomancy, interpreting
moles and birthmarks,
179–81
Monsters, 289–91
Moonlight, cleansing and
charging crystals, 90–91
Moonstone, 37, 65, 74, 85,
109, 126
Morning glory, 160
Muscovite, 85
Mystic cross, 150

N

Narcissus, 160
Negativity, protection from,
263–71
Nettle, 169
Nomancy, 197
Nostradamus, 9, 64
Numerology, 198–233
about: overview and
simplicity of, 198–99
destiny numbers. See
Numerology, birthday
and
personality numbers. See
Numerology, names and

Pythagoras and, 199
Pythagoras and origins
of, 219
Shawn's story, 200
Numerology, angelic, 219–33
combined messages, 230
confusing messages, 231
connecting with angels,
221–33
do's and don'ts, 233
historical perspective on
who angels are, 219–21
messages by number,
222–30
preparing to receive
messages, 231–32
Numerology, birthday and
adding up birth numbers
(calculating destiny
number), 208–9
birthday spell magick,
212–18
destiny numbers (1 to 9)
defined, 209–12
Numerology, names and
adding up name
(calculating personality
number), 208
adding up name numbers
(calculating personality
number), 201–3
number name games, 208
personality numbers (1 to
9) defined, 203–7

O

Oak and oak leaves, 161, 169
Objects, reading people from.
See Psychometry
Obsidian, 64, 74–77, 86,
96–97, 106
Odontomancy, 197

Oinomancy, 197
Onychomancy, 197
Oomancy, 197
Orange (fruit), 162, 184,
267–68
Orchid, 160
Orniscopy, 197
Osiris pendulums, 125
Osteomancy (bone tossing),
173–78
explained, 173–74
historical perspective, 173–74
mixed-bone method, 176
reading bones, 175–77
tossing chicken bones
(bones and their
meanings), 177–78
where to find bones, 174–75
Oval crystal grids, 99–101

P

Palmistry, 140–57
about: overview of, 140–41;
photocopy of hands
for, 141
anecdotes of readings, 151,
156
circle on hand, 155
cross on hand, 155
finger length and
indications, 143
fingernails and indications,
144–45
finger names and
indications, 143–44
grids on hand, 155
hand health and color,
152–53
hand size/shape and, 141–43
historical perspective, 140
initials (letters) and images
on palms, 154–56

Palmistry (cont.)
  love tendencies and hand
    size, 141, 142
  onychomancy and, 197
  patience and perseverance in
    learning, 157
  pentagram on hand, 155
  psychic ritual, 153–54
  square on hand, 155
  star on hand, 155
  unicorn sculptor anecdote,
    151
Palmistry, reading lines, 146–52
  children's lines, 150–51
  fate line, 149–50
  head line, 147–48
  heart line, 146–47
  life line, 148–49
  mystic cross, 150
  relationship lines, 152
  travel lines, 152
Pansy, 160
Pendulum divining, 120–39
  about: overview of, 120–21,
    139
  asking questions, 131–32
  chakra health and, 133–36
  as form of dowsing, 121,
    122, 123
  getting to know your
    pendulum for, 127–29
  health/emotional issues,
    133–36
  history of, 122
  important points to
    remember, 131–32
  predicting sex of unborn
    baby, 122
Pendulums
  about: getting to know
    (how to hold and use),
    127–29

chain length, 123, 127
cleansing and charging,
  137–38
components and structure,
  123, 124
cost considerations, 123, 127
properties and selection,
  123–27
  by stone type and their
    energy qualities, 125–26
  weight of, 124
Pendulums, types/shapes
  chakra, 125
  Merkaba (star-shaped), 124
  Osiris, 125
  sephoroton, 124
  spiral, 124
  triangular, 124
Pentagram on hand, 155
Peony, 160
Personality numbers. See
  Numerology, names and
Pets, Rainbow Bridge and,
  290–92
Phenakite, 86
Phone, scrying with, 80
Plants, psychic power from.
  See Botanomancy
Poppies, 160
Prayer for protection, 290
Precognition, 15, 240
Primrose, 160
Prophecy stone, 86
Protection, prayer and
  incantation for, 290–91
Psychic abilities
  about: overview and
    availability of, 1–3; this
    book and, 2–3; types of,
    overview, 6–7
  availability to develop, 57
  as blessing and curse, 7

children exhibiting, 10–12
enhancing your abilities,
  30–31 (See also Intuition;
  Psychic abilities,
  developing; specific
  abilities)
everyone having, 39
historical perspective, 7–10,
  172–73
kindness and, 293
many forms of, 39
not doubting, 48
opening yourself up to, 2–3
perspective on life and, 293
"psychic" defined, 7–8
scientific research on, 10
as sixth sense, 10–12, 57
spirit guides and, 1–2
Wicca, Wiccans and, 6–7,
  38, 40
Psychic abilities, developing.
  See also ESP; Spells and
  rituals; Telepathy
  about: getting started,
    40–41; opening psychic
    door, 38–39
  assessing your mind and its
    potential (exercises), 41
  believing in your abilities, 48
  crystals for. See Crystals
    references
  external links to sixth sense,
    56–57
  extrasensory training, 41
  imagination and, 45
  learning about different
    abilities, 40–41
  many forms of psychic
    abilities and, 39
  meditation for, 43–45
  reading yourself, 50–52
Psychomancy, 197

Psychometry, 24–26
Puthoff, Harold, 10
Pyramids, crystal, 101–2
Pythagoras, 199, 219

Q

Quartz, 66, 86, 96–97, 100–
    101, *102–4*, 106, 109, 126,
    268, 284. *See also* Amethyst;
    Citrine; Crystal balls; Rose
    quartz; Smoky quartz

R

Rainbow Bridge, 290–92
Readings
    about: aromatherapy for
        clear readings, 164–65
    body language, 52–55
    giving, 55
    tarot, 107–9, 111, 112–19
    of tea leaves, 191–93
    of tossed bones. *See*
        Osteomancy (bone tossing)
    of yourself, 50–52
Reincarnation. *See* Spirit
    guides and reincarnation
Relationship lines, 152
Rhodizite, 86
Rituals. *See specific topics;*
    Spells and rituals
Rosemary, 162, 165
Rose quartz, 65, 126, 232,
    268, 284
Roses, 160–61, 169
Ruby, 126
Ruby kyanite, 86

S

Sage
    properties, 165
    psychic palmistry ritual,
        153–54

smudging with, 88–89, 119,
    270–71
Salt readings (halomancy or
    alomancy), 194–96
Saltwater bath for cleansing
    crystals, 89–90
Sandalwood, 138, 165
Sapphires, 66, 86
Screens, scrying with, 78–80
Scrying. *See also* Crystal balls;
    Mirrors
    about: overview of, 60–61
    crystal enhancement, 65–66
    explained, 61–63
    ganzfeld experiments, 62–63
    history of, 63–65
    interpretation of images, 63
    methods/objects for, 60–61,
        63–64
    reading results, 80–81
    successful session
        expectations, 72
    TV/computer/phone for,
        78–80
Sea salt, cleansing crystals, 90
Selenite, 109, 126
Self, being kind to others
    and, 293
Senses
    clear. *See* Clairalience;
        Clairaudience;
        Claircognizance;
        Clairsentience;
        Clairvoyance
    physical (5), to develop sixth
        sense, 56–57
    sixth, 10–12, 56–57
Sephoroton pendulums, 124
Seraphim, 219
Sixth sense, 10–12, 56–57.
    See also Psychic abilities;
    specific abilities

Sleep. *See* Dreams
Smell, sixth sense
    (clairalience), 12–13
Smoky quartz, 126, 268
Smudging crystals, 88–89
Smudging tarot cards, 110,
    118, 119
Smudging your space, *153–54*,
    270–71
Snowdrop, 161
Sodalite, 86
Souls, stages of development,
    282
Spells and rituals. *See also*
    Meditation
    about: closing rituals, 92;
        empowering crystals for,
        91; general guidelines
        for, 91–92; incorporating
        tarot into spellcasting,
        107; plants for spells (with
        properties), 168–69;
        preparing to connect with
        spirit world, 263; using
        candles in, 91–92
    astral projection, 250–53
    birthday spell magick,
        212–18
    black obsidian mirror
        scrying, 74–77
    crystal field (aura)
        recharging ritual,
        268–69
    crystal grid spell for all-
        seeing, *102–4*
    crystal sleep mask to calm
        dreams, 99
    developing clairvoyance
        with your third eye,
        22–23
    general spell for divining
        with plants, *163–64*

Spells and rituals (*cont.*)
heightening your instincts,
94–95
lucid dreaming, 241–44
psychic magnetic dreaming,
258–59
psychic palmistry ritual,
153–54
ritual bath to cleanse aura
eye, 267–68
smudging your space, 270–71
spell to attract romantic
attention, 184–85
strengthening psychic
abilities, 93–94
Spiral grids, 101
Spiral pendulums, 124
Spirit guides and
reincarnation, 272–81
about: what spirit guides
are, 274
apports to let us know
they're nearby, 278
asking questions of guide,
288
automatic writing and,
287–88
connecting with your spirit
guide, 283–89
hell or no hell, 281
how guides get messages to
us, 277–78
judgment after death and,
280–81
Leanna's story, 272–76
past-life recollection,
274–76
spirit guide Erik and, 271–73
spirit guide Peter and,
274–76, 281, 283, 288
stages of spiritual
development and, 282

what happens when we die,
279–80, 281
where we reincarnate to, 277
why we reincarnate, 277
Spiritual development, stages
of, 282
Spirit world, 262–92. *See
also* Angels; Numerology,
angelic; Spirit guides and
reincarnation
about: overview of, 262
black mirror scrying and,
74, 75, 76–77
connecting with the
cosmos, 271–72
connecting with the dead,
264–65
crystal field (aura)
recharging ritual, 268–69
demons, devils, monsters
and, 289–91
ghosts and, 262
preparing to connect with,
263–71
protection prayer and
incantation, 290–91
ritual bath to cleanse aura
eye, 267–68
smudging your space and,
267–68
Spodomancy, 197
Square on hand, 155
Star on hand, 155
Star-shaped grids, 101
Sunflower, 161
Sunlight, cleansing and
charging crystals, 90–91
Sweet pea, 161

T
Targ, Russell, 10
Tarot magick, 106–19

about: classic deck cards,
107; crystals and, 106;
overview of, 106–7
deck selection, 110
doing readings, 107–9, 111,
112–19
do's and don'ts, 111
five-card spread, 109
horseshoe spread, 109
incorporating into
spellcasting, 107
three-card spread, 108
using two different decks in
spread, 119
Tarot magick, interpreting
cards, 112–19
about: overview of, 112;
using two different
decks in spread, 119
number 0 or 22 (the Fool),
112–13
number 1 (Magician), 113
number 2 (High Priestess),
113
number 5s (of Swords,
Cups, Wands,
Pentacles), 118
number 6 (Lovers,
"Gemini"), 114
number 9 (Hermit,
"Virgo"), 114
number 12 (Hanged Man),
115
number 13 (Death,
"Scorpio"), 115
number 15 (Devil,
"Capricorn"), 116
number 16 (Tower), 116
number 18 (Moon,
"Pisces"), 117
number 20 (Judgement),
117

Tea leaves, reading, 188–94
    about: overview of,
        188–89
    brewing and pouring tea,
        189–91
    diary for tracking readings,
        194
    guidelines for reading,
        191–93
    sample images, words, and
        associations, 192
Tea tree, 165
Tektite, 86
Telepathy
    about, 15
    angels and, 220
    crystal (tektite) for, 86
    defined, 15
    learning to use, 26–29
    testing, 48–49
    value of, 26
Third eye
    chakra affiliations, 135
    developing clairvoyance
        with, 22–23
    opening with magnets,
        256–59
    pineal gland and/as,
        254–55
Thistle, 162

Three-card spread, 108
Tibetan bells, 91, 119
Tiffany stone (purple
    passion), 86
"Time warping," to visit
    different dimensions, 237
Titanium, 86
Topaz (blue), 86
"Topping up" your stone, 92
Travel lines, 152
Triangular pendulums, 124
Tulips, 161
Turquoise, 87, 268–69
TV, scrying using, 78–79

U
Ulexite, 87

V
Vetiver, 165
Violets, 161
Visualization
    astral projection and,
        250–53
    crystals to help with, 84, 87
    death transition and, 280
    dreams and, 242–44
    exercise, for intuition,
        31–32
    plants to help with, 167

value of imagination and, 45
what it is and its benefits,
    242
of white light for prayer
    preparation, 290

W
Warner, William John
    (Cheiro), 140
Water element, cleansing
    pendulum, 137–38
Wax (candle), reading, 186
Wheat, 162
Willow, 162
Wisteria, 161, 162
Writing
    automatic, to channel spirit
        guide, 287–89
    diary for tracking readings,
        194
    dream journal, 33, 244–45

X
Xylomancy, 197

Y
Ylang-ylang, 165

Z
Zygomancy, 197